PLANET GASTRONOMY

100 MOST POPULAR GLOBAL RECIPES

ANANYA BANERJEE

Popular Prakashan
www.popularprakashan.com

Published by Harsha Bhatkal
for Popular Prakashan Pvt. Ltd.
301, Mahalaxmi Chambers
22, Bhulabhai Desai Road
Mumbai 400026
www.popularprakashan.com

First Published 2015

(4411)
ISBN: 978-81-7991-852-4

Photography: Arindam Basu
Food Stylist: Ananya Banerjee
Design: Mahendra Ghanekar

PRINTED IN INDIA
By Saurabh Printers Pvt. Ltd.,
A-16, Sector-IV,
Noida 201301

Author's note

Who wants to eat the same food every day? Should dinner not be different from lunch? At least I would not like to repeat my meals often.

Variety is the spice of life – and our platter is an apt explanation for this expression. Repetition is despised.

It made me wonder how one can have a wide range of the choicest options, when it comes to food! Will it not be wonderful if there was an assortment of admired dishes from across the globe? If a music CD can have a collection of the best songs sung ever, why not food? My desire to taste in my home, the choicest dishes savoured the world over, was yet to be fulfilled.

This led me to the idea of penning down in a book an assortment of the world's most popular dishes.

Once I took an early flight out of Moscow, the temperature was sub-zero, and I had mouth-watering *Blini* (*Russian pancakes*) for breakfast. Flew in to the hot climes of Dubai and savoured a light Middle Eastern *mezze-platter* for lunch at the airport. Took the afternoon flight to London, and relished the famous *fish and chips*.

My frequent travels across the globe took me to the various continents, and enabled me to try authentic local cuisine and learn the cookery tricks-and-tips to reproduce that special taste I craved for.

The world has become smaller and closer. With the advent of television and technology, people travelling beyond their normal boundaries are getting exposed to various places, cultures and most importantly, food.

They say acquired tastes linger better than inborn ones. This has helped intermingling of culinary cultures in recent times. The bland eaters of Europe started fancying spicy Indian curries; and the fiery taste-buds of Indians got acclimatised to the mild, raw food of Japan. The world has literally been brought together on one plate.

With so many diverse tastes beckoning, innumerable curious palates trying beyond the staple fares of our kitchen, is not only a fad, but a necessity too.

The book you are holding will enable you to prepare and enjoy a French *croissant* or Brazilian cheese-bread (*Pao de Queijo*) for breakfast, relish a Thai lunch (*green curry and rice*), relax when the dusk befalls having *Indian chai* (tea) and *Samosas* (pastry with fillings), ending the day with a Moroccan dinner (*chicken tagine with preserved lemons*) or *Australian Macadamia nut-crusted Barramundi*, a nutty fish dish. Needless to mention, ending the treat with the brilliant Italian dessert *Tiramisu* or New Zealand's fresh-fruit *Pavlova* will make the memories of the day satisfying and sweet.

Believe it or not, no cuisine is 'original' in its true sense. Not even French cuisine, the mother of European gastronomy. Italy influenced the visual delight of French food artistry during mid-sixteenth century when

King Henry II married an Italian beauty. Even when Italy is said to have the oldest cookery book, its cuisine is not original, having influences from ancient Greece and the Middle East. The ever popular Mexican dishes are a blend of Spanish influence and Indian spices. Not to talk about the American, Canadian or Australian dishes, which are mostly a fusion of numerous immigrants settled over centuries.

Our cuisines today, are a smörgåsbord of influences from different regions, cultures and ingredients.

Are today's cuisines going to be different tomorrow? The answer is yes. The only constant factor in our lives is change – and our food habits are no different. The famous Italian pastas were not even popular a century back. But in the mid-twentieth century the French brought in the concept of 'Nouvelle cuisine', focussing more on food presentation and retaining the natural flavour of the ingredients by cooking less, significantly changing classical French cuisine.

In spite of the large presence of fast-food restaurants, health and nutrition is increasingly becoming the running rage. Lesser calorie, fat-free and high fibre contents are gaining popularity.

We spend a quarter of our lives thinking, preparing or eating food. This book will make this experience enjoyable and worthwhile.

Can I recreate international cuisine at home?

Yes, you can. It is not difficult at all. When you try a new cooking method, do not be disappointed if you are unsuccessful at your first or second attempts. Try to find what may have gone wrong. In every case, use your own judgement for the time required to cook, quantum of salt, sugar and spice to be used. You may not like the taste of a particular ingredient - drop it. Substitute it with something you like. At the end, if you like the taste of what you have cooked, you are a successful chef.

—Ananya Banerjee
October 2014

Why another cookbook?

There are so many cookbooks in bookstores today, and perhaps in your home too. Why should you buy another one? Don't all cookbooks announce that they are different? Is it not that an average book store contains more recipe books that one can hope to cook in one's lifetime?

The important point of a recipe book is that it needs to work by following simple written instructions. More so, when you are trying out the recipes you may or may not have tasted but have heard a lot about.

I can only say that I have poured my heart into the book you are holding. The recipes work. They are all tested; and tested several times over. Having widely travelled, I had the opportunity to learn about the most popular dishes around the world. This book is an assortment of the choicest recipes of the very best across the globe.

The book is also sprinkled with numerous good-to-know stuff, plenty of tips, kitchen tricks and twists, and a handful of insightful nuggets about the culinary habits of different countries.

Global cuisines will sometimes use ingredients which are not locally available. Substitutes have been suggested wherever I felt that the readers may find it difficult to source a particular ingredient. *Chicken Teriyaki*, a very popular Japanese dish, uses maltose which may be difficult to obtain. Substitute it with honey, and your teriyaki will still be as mouth-watering. The famous *Pecan Pie* of the US naturally uses pecan nuts. If unavailable, substitute with walnuts and enjoy.

For my vegetarian readers, a big challenge could be to try globally popular dishes using meat or fish. Mexican *Chicken Enchiladas* are world famous. Make it with soaked soya mince, and you will be surprised by how tasty this global favourite tastes.

This book is an honest attempt to help all food lovers with a penchant for trying their hand at testing and tasting the best dishes from the world over.

A recipe book is like a guide-book. It provides set formulae. But, depending upon your preferences, taste and local availability of ingredients, subtle changes can be made in most cases. An extra dose of chilli or an additional dash of salt or sugar can make the food more suitable to your very own palate. It is said when baking, follow instruction; when cooking, follow your own taste.

Now enjoy the journey into the enchanting world of the choicest cuisines of the world.

Acknowledgements

This book would not have been possible without the help of a lot of good people. I am truly grateful to all of them but due to paucity of space, I am only mentioning a few.

My mother comes to my mind first. She is the best cook in the world, and I feel I am yet to attain her level of brilliance in cooking. I owe a lot to Robin, my husband. He germinated the first thought in my mind to pen a book on the most popular global recipes, saying that he has never come across any. And lo and behold - it was true. I searched and researched. There was no credible literature available on this subject. He mentored, guided and goaded me throughout the arduous journey. I derive a lot of my strength from my daughter Roshnai, who always tells me that I am the best chef - as usual, the daughter's love for her Mom's food! I am also indebted to my son Abhishek for coining the book title *'Planet Gastronomy'*.

My late father, my guardian angel, who constantly made me believe that 'I am the best in whatever I do' - continues to motivate me in every step I take in my life.

I owe a lot to my friends and family who took the trouble of testing and tasting my recipes. To name a few - Probal Ghosh, Monica Mathur, Debu and Mailee Bhattacharya, Kazi Anirban, Piali Syam, Sanjay and Seema Kapur, Rimjhim Banerjee, Panchali Rakshit, Roopa Kapoor, Zarine Balaporia, Reshma Kulkarni and Dr Manoj Bhatia. I would like to thank my brothers Soumitro, Sudipto and Ruben, sisters Mahasweta, Chandrima and Amrita and nieces Suchismita, Rupsa, Sneha and Sreeja.

My friends, Mehernosh Khajotia, Rachel Lopez and Gautam Saluja, cookery experts and foodies, provided me with guidance and support from time to time. Their advice was golden.

I acknowledge BBC GoodFood, which taught me the value of 'triple-tested' recipes.

I owe special thanks to my friend Antoine Lewis who painstakingly went through the entire manuscript with me to help refine it further.

I would like to express my gratitude to Harsha Bhatkal, my publisher, who took up the gauntlet of publishing this book as soon as he heard of the concept. My sincere thanks to Swapna Shinde, Armaity and the entire team at Popular Prakashan for believing in me and publishing a wonderfully produced book.

CONTENTS

EUROPE

They say, no matter where you travel in Europe, you will never be far from great wine or beer and a hearty meal. Consisting of countries like France, Italy, Germany and Spain, this continent is the home of both traditional and modern cuisine, and is a gourmet's delight. European cuisine is a medley of fresh produce, great dairy products and superb meat and fish resulting in delectable tastes and delightful flavours. The history of European cuisine dates back to the Roman period. Subsequently, with the passage of time, cross-cultural influences have worked together to evolve into European cuisine of today.

AUSTRIA | GERMANY | SWITZERLAND

Austria, a country where Deutsche or German is spoken, has been influenced not only by German cuisine, but also by Spanish, Slovakian, Polish and Swiss cuisines. Apart from *Wiener Schnitzel*, Austria is famous of *Apfelstrudel* (apple filled pastry) and *Sachertorte* (chocolate cake).

Can one think of **German** food without potatoes (*kartoffeln*), sausages (*wurst*) and enormous mugs of beer? While each region of Germany has its own taste, by and large Germany is known as the land of *Sauerkraut* (pickled cabbage), *Sauerbraten* (roasted meat) and *Spaetzle* (homemade noodles). Germans are known to be connoisseurs of good food, with love for fun and cosy gatherings.

The thought of fine chocolates and cheese conjures **Switzerland** in our minds. However chocolate, cheese, and potatoes are not the only food the Swiss have to offer. They are known gastronomes. The French part of Switzerland is known for the world famous *Fondue*. The German part contributed *Roesti* (hashed brown potatoes) and gave the world *muesli*, which many of us have for breakfast even today.

Wiener Schnitzel

Chicken cutlet is popular throughout Germany and Austria (Wien) and originating in Wien – hence the name 'Wiener' schnitzel.

4 chicken breast fillets (in Austria, veil escalope are used)
Salt and pepper to taste
3 tbsp all-purpose flour
2 eggs, beaten
1 cup breadcrumbs
Oil for pan frying

- Cut each fillet vertically into two parts. With the help of a steak hammer, flatten each piece. Season well with salt and pepper.
- Coat the seasoned chicken pieces in flour. Then dip them in beaten egg and subsequently coat them well with breadcrumbs from all sides.
- Heat oil in a pan and fry the schnitzels one by one on medium heat on both sides until golden brown. Cook for about 3 minutes on both sides for the meat inside to cook through.
- Served best piping hot with a cool and refreshing potato salad.

Vegetarian Option: Paneer or cottage cheese steaks can be used instead of the chicken. Season with salt, pepper, green chilli and garlic paste. Coat in a slurry of flour and water, followed by a coating of breadcrumbs. Fry till golden.

Good to know

Health quotient: Chicken breast fillets are the healthiest part of chicken; high in protein; zero fat.

What is escalope: The fillet, which is the boneless piece thinned out, is known as 'escalope' in cooking term. Chicken breast usually provides two 'escalopes'. Turkey breast (when used) provides 5 to 6 'escalopes'.

Tip: Since the spice quotient of the dish is low as nothing except salt and pepper is used, marinating the fillets with green chilli paste, chilli powder, and ginger-garlic paste will be lip-smacking for spice-loving palates.

Makes 8 schnitzels
Preparation skill level: Easy

Stollen

Stollen is a German Christmas specialty. A cross between a cake and bread, it is essentially a yeast dough, with the addition of marzipan and various fruit peels giving it a unique fruitcake texture.

2½ cups or 375 gms flour

1 tbsp active dry yeast

1 tsp sugar

1 cup lukewarm milk

1 egg

⅓ cup or 50 gms castor sugar

⅓ tbsp salt

⅓ cup or 50 gms butter, softened

⅓ cup currants

⅓ cup sultana raisins

⅓ cup red candied cherries, quartered

⅔ cup finely diced candied fruit peels

100 gms marzipan

1 tbsp icing sugar

1 tsp ground cinnamon

Makes 1 large stollen
Preparation skill level: Moderately difficult

- Stir yeast and 1 teaspoon of sugar in lukewarm milk till dissolved. Let it stand for 10 minutes till frothy.
- Add 1 cup of flour in a large bowl. Make a well in the centre; add the frothy yeast milk mixture in the well. Add egg, castor sugar, salt, butter. Add the remaining flour, ¼ cup at a time, stirring well after each addition to form lumpy dough. Transfer the dough onto a floured work platform. Knead well. Incorporate the currants, raisins, dried cherries, and citrus peel. Knead till the dough is smooth. The process should take around 6-7 minutes.
- Place the dough to rest in an oiled bowl. Cover with a damp cloth and leave it to rest in a warm place for an hour or till the dough becomes double its original size.
- Roll the dough into a rectangle. Roll the marzipan into a long cylinder. Place the marzipan in the centre of the dough. Fold from right side like enveloping the marzipan. Again fold over from the left to cover the centre. Press the edges to seal. Place on a baking tray, lined with baking paper. Cover with a damp cloth and let it rise again for 45 minutes or doubled in size.
- Bake in the pre-heated oven at 175°C or 350°F for 10 minutes, and bake for a further 30 to 40 minutes at a reduced temperature of around 150°C. Allow loaf to cool on a wire rack. Dust the cooled loaf with icing sugar, and sprinkle with cinnamon.

Good to know

Enjoy Christmas: Stollen is a perfect alternative to having a traditional cake or pudding during Christmas.

Superb in wintry climes: In Germany it is usually enjoyed with a glass of gluhwein i.e. hot mulled wine spiked with various spices.

Why yeast rises:

- It is a living organism, thriving on natural sugar or starch;
- Combined with moisture and heat, yeast ferments;
- Gas bubbles trapped in the dough or batter makes it rise

Roesti

The signature potato-based dish of Switzerland, usually served with ham, cheese and apple sauce.

500 gms potatoes, grated
½ cup finely chopped onion
Salt and pepper to taste
1 tbsp all-purpose flour
4-6 tbsp oil
1 tbsp Horseradish paste
2 tbsp cream cheese
Rocket leaves to garnish
Ham slices/smoked salmon (optional) (vegetarians can relish roesti with cream cheese and horseradish mixture)
Chives to garnish

- Grate the potatoes coarsely and drain in a sieve to take out excess moisture. Add onions. Season with salt, pepper, and flour.
- In a heavy frying pan, heat 1 tablespoon of oil. Add about 2 heaped tablespoon of potato mixture. Flatten to form a disc of 6 cm. Cook the discs for 2 minutes on each side till brown and crispy. Add 1 tablespoon of oil from the sides to enable browning. Drain.
- Mix horse-radish paste with cream cheese. Garnish with leaves of rocket, ham/smoked salmon and a spoonful of cream cheese mixture. Sprinkle with finely cut chives.

Ananya's Twist

2-3 green chillies and finely chopped coriander leaves may be added to the potato and onion mixture for extra punch.

Makes 2 large or 4 small roesti
Preparation skill level: Easy

FRANCE

French cuisine is often regarded as the alma-mater of European gastronomy. Over the last several decades, French cuisine has undergone several changes. Chef Auguste Escoffier codified modern-day haute cuisine in the 20th century with the 'flavour first' approach. In the 1970s the rise of 'Nouvelle Cuisine' changed everything. Visual appearance took precedence over flavour. In the 1980s, French cuisine turned its course again with traditional cuisine but contemporary presentation, less of cream and butter, more of olive oil (an Italian influence), vegetables and healthy cooking methods like steaming. In a nutshell, France has presented an incredible cultural heritage to the world through its culinary flamboyance.

Quiche Lorraine

A baked pie that is a French classic. A savoury delicacy that finds mention even in 400-year-old cookery books.

1 cup or 150 gms flour, sieved
3 eggs
½ cup or 75 gms chilled cubed butter
Salt and pepper to taste
150 gms smoked bacon rashers or ham, diced
1 stick leek, finely chopped
1 cup fresh cream
Salt and pepper to taste
A pinch of nutmeg

- Place sieved flour into in a work surface. Make a well in the centre.
- Add 1 egg, chilled and cubed butter, salt and pepper into the well. Gradually mix with your fingertips so that the mixture resembles coarse breadcrumbs. It should come together as a lumpy mass. Wrap it in a cling film and refrigerate.

Tip: Do not over-mix. Over-mixing and making a smooth dough will result in a hard pastry later.

- Roll out the dough thinly, sandwiched between two large square sheets of cling-film.
- Lift the rolled dough with the help of the rolling pin and place it onto a quiche dish. Trim the edges with the help of a knife to give it a neat finish.
- 'Blind-bake' the dough in a pre-heated oven at 180˚C or 350˚F for 10-15 minutes.
- Sauté the bacon or ham in a pan. Add the leeks and sauté till soft.
- Take out the semi-baked shell (blind baked) from the oven and spread the sautéed bacon or ham and leeks on the shell.

- Beat the remaining 2 eggs well; add the cream. Season with salt, pepper and nutmeg. Pour the prepared cream mixture over the bacon.
- Bake in a pre-heated oven at 180˚C or 350˚F for 35-40 minutes till eggs are cooked and golden on top. Cut into thick triangles.
- Served best at room temperature, with glass of Champagne or any sparkling wine.

Ananya's Twist

- For vegetarians:

  Sauté sliced zucchini or mushroom (substituting bacon), with olive oil, onion-garlic; stir this mixture to the prepared quiche mixture.

  Substitute eggs with cornflour mixed in cream for the filling.

Serves 4-6
Preparation skill level: Difficult

Good to know

Blind baking: The pastry is baked without any topping so that the bottom of the pastry is cooked well. A cup of beans can be wrapped in aluminium foil and placed on the pastry. The weight of the beans prevent the pastry from rising, yet cooks from the bottom.

Coq au Vin

Chicken (coq) in wine (vin) is a classical French preparation, definitely worth trying.

1 kg chicken, cut into 8 pieces
250 ml red wine
1 carrot
1 stick celery
2 bay leaves
6 black peppercorns
2 cloves garlic, finely chopped
1 sprig thyme
2 tbsp flour
5 tbsp butter
Salt and pepper to taste
70 gms bacon, cut into strips
4 spring onions
1 cup button mushrooms, chopped
1 tbsp parsley, finely chopped

Serves 4
Preparation skill level: Moderate

- Cut the carrots into dices. Roughly chop the celery. Marinate the chicken pieces in the red wine along with carrots, celery, bay leaves, peppercorns, garlic and thyme for 6 hours or preferably overnight.
- Take out the chicken from the marinade and pat dry. Coat the chicken in flour. Heat up 4 tablespoons butter and brown the chicken in it.
- Gradually add all the vegetables from the marinade medium. Add salt and pepper to taste. Pour over the marinade and slow cook the chicken for about one hour in a stove top or a pre-heated oven at 180°C or 350°F.
- Heat up the remaining butter in another pan. Add the bacon, spring onions and mushrooms and sauté for about five minutes.
- Take out the slow cooked chicken from the sauce and arrange it with the mushroom, bacon mixture on a serving plate.
- Reduce the remaining sauce in the pan where chicken was cooked, till thick and pour over the chicken. Garnish with chopped parsley.

Good to know

Due to the red wine marination, the chicken soaks up the colour of the wine and takes on burgundy colour which is a unique characteristic of this dish.

Croissants

Flaky, buttery pastry, popular world over.

3⅓ cups or 500 gms all-purpose flour; keep some extra for rolling out

2⅓ cups or 350 gms unsalted butter

1½ cups or 320 ml milk

2 tsp quick rising yeast

2 tbsp sugar

1 tsp salt

1 beaten egg

- Heat the milk to lukewarm. Add yeast, 1 tablespoon flour and sugar to the milk. Stir till dissolved. Keep aside till bubbles form on the surface of the milk.
- Sift flour and salt and place in a large bowl. Make a well in the centre and add the yeast mixture. Bring the dry (i.e. flour and salt) and wet (i.e. milk-mixture) ingredients together to form a soft, lumpy dough.
- Tip the mixture onto a large work place and knead for 5 minutes into a smooth and elastic dough. Cover and

keep for 1-hour, in an oiled bowl three times the size of the dough. Place it in a warm place till the dough is double its original size (the yeast in the dough helps it to rise). Keep aside.

- Roll the chilled butter between two large sheets of grease-proof baking paper to a rectangle approximately 8 x 4 inches.
- Take the risen dough, punch it down to get rid of excess air and roll in to a rectangle of about 16 x 5 inches (the dough should be twice as long as the rolled butter and little more in width). Place the butter on one side of the length of the dough, and then envelope the butter with the other half of the uncovered dough. This will enclose the butter fully, with the dough. Roll out the dough with the butter sandwiched in between, into a little larger rectangle. Mentally divide the dough into three parts. Then, fold it like a three-part folder letter. This means fold one-third of the rectangular dough, then fold the other one-third, such that it overlaps the earlier folded part. Chill and repeat this procedure of rolling and folding, twice more ie. three times.
- Divide the dough into two parts. Roll out into two large rectangles. Using a triangle template, cut out the rolled dough into triangles. Each part will provide 6 triangles making 12 in total.
- Roll each triangle, starting from the large end. Bend the two sides slightly. This will form the crescent shape.
- Brush with beaten eggs. Chill overnight.
- Before baking, remove from the refrigerator and let the croissants double in size. Brush with beaten eggs again and bake in a pre-heated oven at 200°C or 400°F for 15-20 minutes or until the crust is golden brown.

Vegetarian option: Instead of brushing the croissant with eggs, brush with milk for a similar shine.

Makes 12 croissants
Preparation skill level: Difficult

Chocolate Éclairs

A small log-shaped bun made of choux paste (a type of pastry dough) filled with cream and coated with chocolate icing.

For the choux pastry

1 cup or 150 gms all-purpose flour

1 cup or 250 ml water

5 tbsp or 50 gms butter

Salt to taste

1 tsp sugar

2 eggs

1 egg for egg wash

For the filling

1 cup milk

A few drops of vanilla essence

3 egg yolks

2 tbsp sugar

1 tbsp cornflour

1 tbsp butter

For the chocolate glaze

1 cup chopped dark chocolate

½ cup heavy cream

For the choux pastry

- In a large saucepan, bring the water, butter and salt to a boil. Take the pan off the heat and stir in the flour and sugar with a wooden spoon till incorporated. Return to the heat and cook -stirring, till the flour forms a ball and pulls away from the side of the pan. Take the pan off the heat. Add eggs, one at a time. Mix well until the dough is smooth and glossy and the eggs are completely incorporated. (Tip: The dough should be thick, and drop off the spoon easily when shaken.)
- Pour dough into a piping bag (a cone-shaped hand-held cake decoration bags). Line a baking tray with parchment paper. Pipe (using the piping bag) fat lengths of dough (about the size and shape of a hot dog) onto the lined baking tray, leaving 2 inches of space between them. Brush with egg-wash. Bake in a pre-heated oven at 200°C or 400°F for 30 minutes or till the choux buns are golden brown.

For the filling

- Heat the milk in a pan. Add vanilla essence and boil over medium heat. Set aside.
- In a bowl, whisk the egg yolks and sugar until light and fluffy. Add the cornflour and whisk until no lumps remain. Add the mixture to the boiled milk.
- Cook over medium-high heat, whisking constantly, until thickened. Remove from the heat and stir in the butter and refrigerate the custard for further use. (Tip: The custard can be made up to 24 hours in advance.)

For the glaze

- Heat the cream just until it boils. Take it off the heat.
- Add the chopped chocolate and whisk until melted and smooth. Set aside. (Tip: The glaze can be made up to 48 hours in advance. Cover and refrigerate until ready to use, and reheat in a microwave or over a pan of hot water when ready to use.)

Ananya's Twist

Left over choux-paste dough can be deep-fried and served with the chocolate glaze prepared in this recipe. This deep-fried dough is called 'churros', a popular Mexican-Spanish dessert.

Makes 8-10 éclairs
Preparation skill level: Difficult

Good to know

Once you have learnt the method of making choux pastry, you will be able to make profiteroles and croquembouche, which has similar techniques.

For assembling

- Transfer the prepared filling to a piping bag fitted with a nozzle. Pierce the underside of each éclair with the tip of the nozzle, gently squirting a little of the filling into the éclair.
- Dip the tops of the éclairs in the warm chocolate glaze and set aside. Best served chilled.

Crêpe Suzette

Pancakes in an orange boozy-sauce! A classic French dessert.

1 cup or 150 gms flour
½ cup or 125 ml fresh orange juice
2 tbsp orange zest
4-5 tbsp orange liqueur
1 cup or 150 gms sugar
½ cup or 150 gms butter
¾ cup or 200 ml milk
¾ cup or 200 ml water
3 egg yolks
2 tbsp Cognac
2-3 pieces of star anise to decorate

Good to know

- **Flaming flambé:** Igniting with alcohol is known as flambéing. The dessert looks particularly attractive when flambéed as it is served with a pale blue flame because of the burning alcohol.
- **All about pans:** Crêpe pans are usually made in cast-iron. These pans are great conductor of heat and cooks food evenly. Once the pan is proved or seasoned, the surface acts as a non-stick.

Vegetarian option: Follow the same recipe, but omit the eggs.

- Mix ½ cup of sugar, orange zest and 5 tablespoons of melted butter well. Add ½ cup of fresh orange juice and 2 tablespoons of orange liqueur and mix well. Cover and refrigerate.
- To prepare the pancake mixture, place milk, water, egg yolks, ½ cup sugar, 1 tablespoon of the orange liqueur, flour and 5 tablespoons of melted butter in a bowl and whisk well to form a batter of pouring consistency. Cover and refrigerate for at least 2 hours.
- Rub a skillet or a heavy bottomed pan with butter. Pour about ¼ cup measure of batter on the pan. Spread it evenly on the pan to form pancakes. Cook one pancake at the time over moderate heat. Keep aside. Continue the process till all the pancakes are made.
- Heat the refrigerated orange mixture for one minute on the skillet. Place one pancake in the orange mixture. Turn it over and fold it in half, and then half again to form triangles. Continue the same process with the other pancakes.
- Heat 2 tablespoons of Cognac and 2 tablespoons of orange-liqueur in a saucepan. Pour over pancakes. Ignite - cautiously - with a match and serve immediately, decorated with star anise.

Tip:

When zesting (removal of the outer layer) an orange or lemon, be careful not to reach the white pith of the fruit. The top layer of citrus fruits contains the essential oil and all the flavour but the white pith is extremely bitter.

Serves 4
Preparation skill level: Moderate

ITALY

Italian cuisine is much more than just pizzas and pastas. It is the freshness of ingredients which is the character of its cuisine. Ingredients used are never too many but are farm-fresh. No masking, no additional sauces and spices. It's the original flavour of meat, or tomatoes or any other fresh ingredients, which will linger on one's palate for a long time. Italy's contribution to the world includes *risotto* (rice dish), *tiramisu* (dessert), *gnocchi* (potato dumplings), and *prosciutto* (cured ham). The list is unending, including famous cheeses like *mozzarella* and *Parmigiano-Reggiano*. Italy is truly a gastronome's heaven.

Lasagne

A baked and layered pasta dish, alternating between layers of cheese and sauce. A Southern Italian classic, known to be the world's oldest pasta-preparation.

6 sheets of 'no cook' lasagne
250 gms lamb mince (vegetarians can use soya mince instead of lamb)
2 tbsp olive oil
½ cup onion, chopped
1 tbsp garlic, minced
½ cup grated carrots
1 bay leaf
2 pinches dried oregano
1 tbsp Worcestershire sauce
Salt and freshly ground black pepper to taste
1 tbsp tomato purée
2 tbsp red wine (optional)
1 cup tomatoes, chopped
¼ cup cream

For the sauce

2½ tbsp butter
2½ tbsp all-purpose flour
1¼ cups milk
Salt and pepper to taste

- Heat oil and sauté the onions, garlic and carrots. Add bay leaf, a pinch of oregano, Worcestershire sauce and salt and pepper to taste. Sauté till onions are soft.
- Add the meat and the tomato purée and mix well. Continue to sauté until the meat browns nicely. Add the wine and cook off the alcohol. Add the tomatoes. Simmer for a further 2-3 minutes. Finally add the cream, turn off the heat and set aside.

For the sauce

- Melt the butter in a saucepan. Add the flour. Stir briskly till the raw smell of the flour disappears. Add a third of the milk, whisking to prevent any lumps forming. Add the rest of the milk .little by little, whisking as you go. Season with salt, pepper and nutmeg.
- Let the sauce to cook for a minute. Add the Cheddar cheese. Stir well and keep aside.

For layering the lasagne

- Evenly spread half of the meat sauce on the bottom of the baking dish and place pasta sheets on top (break the sheets if necessary to avoid any overlapping). Then pour 3 tablespoons of the cheese sauce, spreading evenly with help of a spatula. Spoon the remaining meat on top. Add the final layer of pasta and then use the spatula to pour over the remaining cheese sauce.

Pinch of ground nutmeg

6 tbsp grated Cheddar cheese

3 tbsp grated Parmesan cheese

Serves 4
Preparation skill level: Moderate

- Sprinkle grated Parmesan and oregano. Bake in a pre-heated oven at 220°C or 425°F for 20-25 minutes, or until the cheese is golden brown and bubbling.

Vegetarian option: Replace lamb-mince, with mince of sundry vegetables like carrot, beans, cabbage and cauliflower.

Pizza Margherita

A basic pizza topped with tomato sauce and mozzarella cheese, believed to have derived its name from the Italian queen Margherita.

For the pizza base

2⅓ cups flour

2 tsp active dry yeast

1 cup lukewarm water

1 tbsp olive oil plus extra for drizzling

1 tsp salt

For the tomato sauce

4 tbsp passata or readymade Italian tomato paste (Possible substitute: Thickened tomato paste)

Handful of fresh basil

1 tsp garlic, minced

Salt and pepper to taste

For the topping

2 balls (50 gms each) fresh mozzarella cheese, sliced

Handful basil leaves

1 tsp oregano, dried

Makes 2 large pizzas or 4 small pizzas
Preparation skill level: Moderate

For the pizza base

- Stir the yeast in the lukewarm water and olive oil. Keep it aside till bubbles form on the surface (this is due to the activation of yeast).
- Add salt to the flour in a large bowl. Make a well, in the centre. Pour the yeast mixture and bring the dough together with a wooden spoon till soft and lumpy dough forms. Turn the dough onto a lightly floured surface and knead for 5 minutes until smooth and elastic.
- Cover the dough with a cling wrap and set aside. (Tip: for making a thin crust, proving the dough i.e. leaving the dough aside till it is almost double its original size, is not required like other bread preparation.)

For the tomato sauce

- Mix the passata, basil and garlic together, season with salt and pepper. This sauce is to spread on the base.

For assembling

- Divide the dough into four parts. Roll out the dough into large discs (pizza base) of about 12 cm diameters each. (Tip: The dough needs to be very thin as it will rise in the oven.)
- Place the pizza base onto floured baking sheets.
- Spread the prepared sauce over bases with the back of a spoon. Sprinkle with sliced mozzarella cheese and drizzle with olive oil. Bake in a pre-heated oven at 240°C or 475°F for 8-10 minutes until crisp.
- Serve with a drizzle of olive oil, fresh basil and dried oregano.

Tiramisu

Coffee-flavoured layered dessert, alternating between mascarpone cheese and sponge-finger. A very popular Italian dessert which literally means 'pick me up'.

24 packaged ladyfingers or sponge fingers (Possible substitute: 2 inch strips of sponge cake)

500 gms mascarpone cheese

2 cups strong black coffee, cooled

6 egg yolks (Tip: since this recipe uses raw eggs, ensure they are farm fresh)

3 tbsp sugar

2 tbsp dark rum/Amaretto liqueur/ Cointreau/Marsala wine (optional)

½ cup bittersweet chocolate shavings, or 2 tbsp cocoa powder for garnish

- Beat egg yolks and sugar until thick and pale. Add mascarpone cheese and beat until smooth.
- In a shallow platter, add black coffee and coffee liqueur, if using. Dip each ladyfinger into the coffee for only 5 seconds. (Tip: Don't allow the ladyfingers to soak too long or they will fall apart). Place the soaked ladyfinger on a square or a rectangular baking dish, breaking them in half if necessary in order to fit the bottom of the dish.
- Spread evenly half of the mascarpone mixture over the ladyfingers. Arrange another layer of espresso soaked ladyfingers and top with remaining mascarpone mixture. Similarly a few more layers of ladyfingers and mascarpone mixture can be repeated.
- Cover and refrigerate for at least 2 hours, and up to 8 hours to set well.
- Sprinkle with chocolate shavings or dust cocoa powder through a fine sieve to cover the surface of the tiramisu just before serving.

Tip: Sprinkling of cocoa powder before hand darkens the colour of the cocoa. It is advisable to dust with it just before serving.

Vegetarian option: To make it eggless, the cream mixture can be made by beating mascarpone cheese with double cream and sugar, instead of the eggs. The rest of the recipe will be the same.

Recipe yield: Serves 4-6
Preparation skill level: Moderate

Ananya's Twist

Instead of the conventional coffee flavour, tiramisu can be made in strawberry, raspberry, mango and peach flavour. The coffee and liquor decoction has to be substituted with the respective fruit juice and rum (if using). Instead of the cocoa powder, fresh fruits can be added on top as well as layered inside.

Peas and Asparagus Risotto

A creamy rice dish cooked in an aromatic broth and wine – an Italian classic.

1 cup Arborio rice

4-5 asparagus spears, (each cut into 4 pieces lengthwise)

1 litre chicken stock

1 tbsp olive oil

1 medium onion, finely chopped

1 tsp garlic, minced

½ cup dry white wine

1 cup peas

⅓ cup finely grated Parmesan cheese

2 tbsp butter, chopped

Salt and pepper to taste

Parmesan cheese shavings to garnish

Good to know

- Arborio is risotto rice from Italy. It can be substituted by a local produce but results will be different.
- Asparagus is known to be an aphrodisiac; Greeks even offer these to the Gods.

Serves 4
Preparation skill level: Moderate

- Put the chicken stock to boil. Simmer under low heat. (Tip: Make sure the stock is simmering while you prepare the dish.)
- Heat oil in a pan. Add onion and garlic. Cook till onions are soft. Add rice and cook till each grain of rice is coated with oil and it acquires a nutty aroma. (Tip: Arborio rice should be given only a light rinse; or else the starch will be washed away with water; it is better to avoid rinsing the rice at all, to prevent losing the starch, as the starch helps the Risotto to be creamy.)
- Add wine and on a medium to low heat bring it to boil until wine is reduced by half.
- Add ½ cup of stock to rice mixture. Cook, stirring, until stock has been absorbed. Repeat this process with the remaining stock. (Tip: Remember to add one ladleful of stock at a time. This renders the creamy and smooth texture of the risotto.)
- Before adding the last cup of stock, add the peas and asparagus to rice mixture, reserving a few asparagus heads for garnish.
- Cook for 5 minutes. Add the cheese and butter. Season with salt and pepper. Serve garnished with cheese.

Vegetarian options: You can be creative with the choice of vegetables. Instead of peas and asparagus, you may use French beans, beetroot purée, or mushrooms.

Non-vegetarian options: With or without the vegetables, you can use chicken, diced white fish or shrimps, for different tastes and flavours.

Ananya's Twist:

- Additions of chopped nuts, raisins or diced apples, can perk up the taste of the risotto.
- Arancini: Left-over Risotto can be mixed with beaten eggs, formed into balls, coated in breadcrumbs, and deep-fried. This will help to make a very popular Italian snack – *Arancini*.

SPAIN

Spanish cuisine has retained its simplicity through centuries, giving robust and rustic flavours to its dishes. The dishes are rather uncomplicated and are produced from locally available ingredients. Garlic and olive oil are basic ingredients for Spanish food. Spain is the world's largest producer of olive oil. Ham or *Jamon* is a Spaniards' pride and they make the finest ham dishes. *Chorizo*, a pork sausage made with paprika, is most loved. To top it all, who has not heard of *tapas* - an array of appetisers, or tapas bars, the home of tit-bit eats and superb wine?

Paella

A rice dish, containing an array of seafood, meat, *chorizo* and vegetables, flavoured with saffron - the Spanish national dish, originating in *Valencia*, eastern Spain.

1 cup of Arborio rice (*Arborio*, an Italian rice is more easily available. Paella is usually made of Spanish rice *bomba* or *calaspara*)
5-6 large shrimps
3-4 pieces of chicken thighs and legs
100 gms sliced chorizo sausages
1 cup clams, mussels and calamari (optional)
½ cup olive oil
1 tsp garlic, minced
½ cup chopped onion
½ cup capsicum (all colours), cut into thick strips
2 tbsp tomato paste
1 tsp sugar
1 tbsp paprika
2 tbsp chopped fresh parsley
1 tsp dried thyme
Salt to taste
Few strands of saffron
2½ cups chicken stock

- Heat oil in a Paella pan. (Good-to-know: Paella gets its name from a flat-based frying pan with two handles, used as the cooking vessel.) (Substitute for Paella pan: Any frying pan.)
- Brown the chorizo over high heat for 1-2 minutes. (Good-to-know: Chorizo contains high amount of paprika; rendering bright red colour and flavour to the oil.)
- Add the chicken, sear for 2-3 minutes. Remove the chicken and chorizo and keep aside.
- In the same pan add garlic, onion and capsicum and cook till *al dente* (cooked but still firm to the bite). Remove from the pan and keep aside.
- Add rice to the pan. Stir till the rice browns. Add tomato paste. Caramelise it by sprinkling sugar and sauté on high heat. Add the kept aside vegetables, chicken and chorizo back in the pan.
- Dissolve saffron in 2 teaspoons of warm water and pour it on the rice. (Good-to-know: Saffron is world's most expensive spice; it's a stigma or thread of a flower, handpicked and dried.) (Tip: Heat releases the flavour and essence of saffron. Dissolving in hot water or milk will release the hue and the aroma.)
- When the rice is slightly translucent add warm chicken stock to cover the whole mixture. (Tip: This step is extremely important. Ideally it should be stirred a few times, initially for

Good to know

- Essentials and optional: Paella's four essential ingredients are: Spanish rice, onions, pimento and saffron. To provide variation, you may add any one or all of the following: fried chicken, ham, pork, chorizo sausage, mussels, clams, and prawns. For special occasions, you can use lobsters
- Mussels – open and shut case: If using mussels, it should be checked that they are all closed, before cooking. Open or half-opened mussels should be discarded. On the contrary, after being cooked, each and every mussel should open up. In case any mussel remains closed, it should be discarded.

5-10 minutes, adding stock bit by bit till the rice absorbs all the stock and adjust seasoning. Then for the next 10-20 minutes it should be left alone to cook. Don't worry about rice burning to the bottom; in fact the crispy burnt part is savoured as a delicacy in Spain.)

- Once the paella is stirred for the last time cook further for 15 minutes, place the shrimp (clams, mussels, calamari if using) on top, turning over after 2-4 minutes to cook other side.
- If the rice on top still seems to be *al dente*, cover and let it sit for another 20 minutes. Then it will be perfect. Garnish with lemon wedges.

Vegetarian Option:

Omit all the sea-food, chicken and the chorizo. Along with the tri-coloured capsicums, add soya chunks, pine nuts, and zucchini and follow the rest of the recipe.

Serves 4
Preparation skill level: Moderate

Gambas Ajillo

Sizzling garlic prawns - An all-time favourite tapas dish.

400 gms (20 medium sized) shrimp, shelled, deveined and tails intact

4 large cloves garlic, finely minced

4 tbsp extra virgin olive oil

1 tsp red pepper flakes

Juice of 1 lemon

1 tsp sweet Spanish paprika (Possible alternative: Powdered Kashmiri red chillies; provides colour but with less pungency)

6 tbsp (¼ cup) Cognac or dry sherry (optional)

Salt and pepper to taste

3 tsp chopped fresh parsley

3-4 basil leaves

Good to know

- De-vein intestinal vein of prawns: Most prawns have a black intestinal vein running along its back. This is ugly and unpleasant to eat. It should ideally be removed before cooking.

Serves 4

Preparation skill level: Very easy

- Warm olive oil in a pan over medium heat. Add the garlic and red pepper flakes and sauté for a minute.
- Increasing the flame to high heat. Immediately add the shrimp, lemon juice, sherry or Cognac and paprika. Stir well and sauté until the shrimp turns pink and curls up. The process will take about 3 minutes.
- Transfer the shrimp along with the oil and sauce to a plate or serve right from the pan.
- Season to taste with salt and freshly ground black pepper. Sprinkle with parsley and basil leaves.
- Best served with crusty bread to mop up the delicious gravy.

Gazpacho

A refreshing cold soup, a thirst quencher, to beat the summer heat. Also known as liquid salad.

500 gms ripe tomatoes, peeled, de-seeded, and coarsely chopped

2 slices of white bread, crust removed

2 cucumbers, peeled, de-seeded, and coarsely chopped

1 small red onion, coarsely chopped

1 tbsp minced garlic

2 green capsicums

6 tbsp extra virgin olive oil

3 tbsp red wine vinegar

Salt and pepper to taste

Few sticks of celery to garnish

- Soak the bread in water. Squeeze for a minute. Remove and squeeze dry.
- Blend the tomatoes, bread, cucumbers, onions, garlic and capsicums in a blender, to a smooth purée.
- Add oil and vinegar to the blended purée or gazpacho. Season with salt and pepper to taste. Mix well. Cover and refrigerate for at least 1 hour. Serve cold with celery sticks.

Tip:

Gazpacho, which is enjoyed chilled, can be served in shot-glasses, with a celery stick and dash of extra-virgin olive oil and a few ice cubes.

The easiest way to peel tomatoes is to drop them into boiling water and place the tomatoes into the cold water for 1 minute. Carefully remove the tomatoes. The skin will peel-off easily.

Serves 4-6
Preparation skill level: Easy

ENGLAND | SCOTLAND | IRELAND

Scotch, the most famous whisky is **Scotland's** gift to the world. **Ireland** has not been left far behind, with their contribution of Irish beer and the renowned liqueur – Bailey's Irish Cream. **English** cuisine however has been vastly influenced by several regions of the world, as a result of colonialism and immigration. The British take pride in their curries and chutneys, a characteristic cuisine from the Indian subcontinent. Mashed potatoes, pies and sausages are all typically British, with fish-n-chips being exclusively English. A culinary high point and a ritual in the region is its afternoon tea, served in the finest porcelain wares with the choicest snacks.

Fish and Chips

Batter fried cod or haddock served along with French fries, and malt vinegar—favourite street food of Britain.

For the fish

500 gms firm-fleshed white fish fillets

2 cups all-purpose flour

1 tbsp baking powder

1 tsp salt

1/4 tsp chilli powder

1 cup chilled beer

3 tbsp cornflour, for dredging

For the chips

4 large potatoes

1 litre vegetable oil

Salt to taste

For the chips

- Cut potatoes in the shape of French fries. Wash and drain potatoes. Blanch in hot water for 3 minutes. Drain well and then fry the potatoes in small batches in hot oil for 2 to 3 minutes until they are pale and floppy. Remove from oil, drain and cool to room temperature.
- Reheat oil and re-immerse fries and cook until crisp and golden brown, about 2 to 3 minutes. Remove and drain on roasting rack. Season with salt while hot. (Tip: Cooking the potatoes thrice i.e. once blanching and twice frying produces super crisp fries from outside and crumbly and soft from inside.)

For the fish

- Mix the flour, baking powder, salt and chilli powder well. Add beer, and whisk until the batter is completely smooth and free of any lumps. Chill for 15 minutes. (Good-to-know: The batter can be made earlier but not more than one hour ahead of use.)
- Heat the remaining oil. Lightly dredge the fish fillets in cornflour. Dip the fish into batter and immerse into hot oil, few fillets at a time. Deep-fry the fish until golden brown on both sides. This process may take about 2 minutes. Drain the fish on a wire rack to get rid of the excess oil. Serve with the prepared chips.

Tip:

Oil to be clean tasting – odourless, refined oil.

Serves 2-3
Preparation skill level: Easy

Good to know

Fishy oil tests:

- Ideal temperature from frying a batter coated or batter fried fish could be 180˚C - 190˚C.
- To test the ideal temperature of oil, in which fish would be deep-fried.
    - Drop a cube of white bread; in 30 seconds the bread should turn golden brown; or ensure that the oil is hot enough: Any portion of batter coming in contact with the oil, puffs up.

English Trifle

An English dessert usually layered with fruits, custard, jelly, cream and spiked with sherry or rum.

400 gms strawberry Swiss roll (can be obtained off the shelf. If unavailable use sponge cake and strawberry jam)

1 packet ready jelly crystal (e.g. Kraft's Jell-O)

2 cups prepared vanilla custard (custard to have pouring consistency)

2 cups sliced strawberries or blueberries, or mixed fruit

2 cups whipped cream

4 tbsp rum or sherry (optional)

Handful of cherries

Few almond flakes or shaved chocolate to garnish

Ananya's twist:

- This recipe can have a number of variations. Addition or omission of different fruits, both seasonal and canned can give a varied taste.
- Instead of Swiss rolls, you may use sponge cakes, biscuits, or different types of cakes, to bring variations.
- Instead of gin, sherry or dark rum can be added.
- Alcohol can be replaced with orange juice.

Serves 6
Preparation skill level: Easy

- Follow the packet instruction for making jelly. Normally it is made by adding boiling water to the jelly crystals till dissolved. Then it is chilled for 4-5 hours till set or jelly forms. (Ananya's Twist: Add 4 tablespoons of gin while making the jelly, it will give a unique flavour.) Once set, cut into cubes and keep aside.
- Arrange 4 tablespoons custard on a big glass bowl or 4-6 individual glass bowls. (Tip: usually served in glass bowls so that the layering of various fruits, custard, can be seen through and looks pretty.) Arrange the Swiss rolls layered on the side wall of the glass bowl, creating a hollow in the middle. Sprinkle 2 tablespoons of rum on the rolls. Put in the hollow, bananas, strawberries or other fruits, and cut jelly cubes. Cover this up by pouring 4-5 tablespoons of custard.
- Repeat the process again by creating another layer of Swiss rolls spiked with the remaining rum, followed by fruits, jelly and custard.
- Top the final layer with whipped cream.
- Garnish with cherries or toasted almond flakes or chocolate shavings.

Vegetarian option: Use eggless sponge or Swiss rolls to make this completely eggless.

Scottish Shortbread

A classic, crumbly, melt-in-the-mouth biscuit, known as the 'jewel in the crown' of Scottish baking.

1½ cups or 225 gms butter (if the butter is unsalted add a pinch of salt)

½ cup + 3 tbsp or 110 gms fine castor sugar, plus extra for sprinkling

1½ cups or 225 gms all-purpose flour, plus extra for dusting

2 tbsp cornflour

Makes 12 shortbreads
Preparation skill level: Easy

- Cream the butter, and sugar, until light, fluffy and pale in colour.
- Sieve the flour and cornflour into the bowl of butter and sugar. Mix quickly and thoroughly to bring all the ingredients together, without over mixing.
- Tip the mixture onto a lightly floured work surface and begin kneading lightly and quickly to form a loose dough.
- Roll out the dough between 2 sheets of baking paper to ¼ inch i.e. 1 cm thick. Remove the top sheet of paper. Prick the surface all over with a fork. Cut into rounds using a cookie cutter. Place the Scottish shortbreads on a lightly greased baking sheet and bake for 25-30 minutes in a pre-heated oven at 170°C or 325°F, or until pale brown and crisp. Leave to cool on a cooling rack.
- Store in an airtight tin or box. Serve with fresh cut fruits and fresh-cream or ice-cream as a dessert. Can also be enjoyed with tea or coffee.

Irish Stew

Hearty lamb and vegetable stew synonymous with Irish cooking.

500 gms mutton/lamb with bones cut into chunks

2-3 large potatoes, peeled and quartered

1 tsp butter

1 tsp oil

2 tbsp flour

1 tbsp celery, finely chopped

2 onions, cut into chunks

1 tsp garlic, minced

1 cup carrots, cut into large sticks

Salt and pepper to taste

4 cups chicken stock or lamb stock (can use store-bought stock or prepared stock at home)

1 cup milk

½ tsp fresh thyme leaves

1 tbsp chopped fresh parsley

Serves 2
Preparation skill level: Easy

- Heat butter and oil in a pan; add the flour and sauté till raw smell of the flour disappears. Add the lamb to the flour. Sauté well.
- Add the celery, potatoes, onions, garlic, carrots, and salt and pepper to the lamb. Pour in the stock, and bring to the boil. Add the milk, thyme and parsley and mix well, reserving some parsley leaves for garnish.
- Pressure cook the lamb for 15-20 minutes over medium heat or place the lamb in a baking dish and bake in a pre-heated oven at 170°C or 325°F, for 1½ hours. Garnish and serve.

Tip:

Stock can be prepared at home by boiling meat trimmings and bones in plenty of water for 2 hours and strained to use.

Good to know

- **Irish-stew and potatoes:** Potatoes were the staple food for the Irish up-to the 19th century. In 1845 the potato harvest failed, and famine followed. As a result the Irish broadened their cultivation and grew more varieties of crops on their fertile soil. The famous Irish stew, which was earlier made of potatoes, was added with lamb and vegetables.

Vegetarian option:

You can go meatless. Use more vegetables like squash and beans to make a vegetable stew.

BELGIUM

Belgium, this tiny country's cuisine is often over-shadowed by its very famous gastronomic neighbour France. Belgian chocolates, waffles and beer are world famous. But, nothing beats *Moules-Frites*, a bowl of mussels with Belgian potato fries, and it is something to die for. France (Wallonian cooking) and Netherlands (Flemish cuisine) have influenced this country's food, which is good and simple.

Waffles

Waffles are cooked in a 'waffle-iron' (a waffle making appliance) to give it a distinctive honey-combed or check-patterned impression. Belgian waffles are known world over and are usually served dusted with confectioner's sugar, melted butter, honey or topped with chocolate, soft fruits or whipped cream.

1 cup all-purpose flour
1 tbsp sugar
1½ tsp baking powder
1 pinch salt
1 cup milk or 1½ cups buttermilk
2 eggs
2 tbsp melted butter

3-4 small waffles
Preparation skill level: Moderately easy

- Mix flour, sugar, baking powder, and salt; in a bowl. Keep aside.
- Whisk milk and eggs and melted butter well and pour over the flour, sugar mixture. Beat well to a smooth batter. Pour in the melted butter. Mix well.
- Heat and grease the waffle iron. Pour a generous ½ cup of batter into the centre, spreading it evenly. Cook the waffle for 2 to 3 minutes or till brown and crisp.
- Serve warm with a dusting of icing sugar, or butter and maple syrup, or with strawberries and cream.

Tips:

- Crispy-waffles: For extra crisp waffles, add 1-2 tablespoons oil to the batter. The oil will also help the waffles from sticking to the surface of the pan.
- Butter-milk works: Substituting milk with butter-milk will produce tender and delicate waffles.
- Make old into new: Best way to reheat already prepared waffles, popping them in a toaster. It will taste almost freshly made.

GREECE

Greek cuisine is synonymous with Mediterranean gastronomy. The freshest catch from the sea and unsullied vegetables are typical ingredients for Greek cooking. The locally grown kalamata olives (dark and plump looking) are used in stews, appetisers and salads, apart from being squeezed to produce olive oil. Greece has also given brilliant cheeses to the world – *feta* and *halumi*. A Greek meal cannot be complete without the taste of *moussaka*, a layered baked dish of mince meat, eggplants and cheese sauce; and a cool cucumber-yoghurt dip called *tzatziki*.

Moussaka

Oven baked dish made with layers of eggplant slices,
potatoes and a meat sauce, topped with a thick béchamel sauce.

1 large eggplant
500 gms or 2 cups lamb, minced
1 large potato, boiled and sliced
Salt and pepper to taste
4 egg whites, lightly beaten (reserve yolks for béchamel)
4 tbsp olive oil
1 cup chopped onions
2 tbsp minced garlic
½ cup red wine (optional)
¼ tsp allspice powder (Possible substitute: Use all-purpose seasonings)
¼ cup chopped fresh parsley
2 tbsp tomato paste
1 cup fresh puréed tomato
1 tsp sugar
½ cup breadcrumbs
1 cup grated Kefalotyri (a typical Greek cheese) or Parmesan cheese

- Slice the eggplant into ½ inch slices. Sprinkle enough salt and rest them for 10 minutes. This process will enable bitter juices to accumulate out of the eggplant. Rinse and pat dry. Dip each of the eggplant slices in the beaten egg whites and then dredge them in the breadcrumbs to coat well from all sides. Pan-fry the eggplants in olive oil till golden. Keep aside.
- Heat 2 tablespoons olive oil in a pan. Brown the lamb mince in a pan till seared. Add onion and garlic and sauté well for 5 minutes until fragrant. Add wine to pan to deglaze and allow it to simmer and reduce till alcohol evaporates. Add allspice, parsley, tomato paste, puréed tomatoes, and sugar and simmer uncovered till the excess liquid evaporates.

For the béchamel sauce

- Melt butter over low heat, add flour and cook till the raw smell of flour evaporates. Add milk to mixture in a steady stream, whisking continuously. Simmer over low heat till thick. remove from heat.
- Stir in beaten egg yolks and pinch of nutmeg. Return to heat and stir until sauce thickens.

For the béchamel sauce

½ cup flour

½ cup butter

2 cups warm milk

4 egg yolks, lightly beaten

Pinch of grated nutmeg

Vegetarian option: Use soya mince instead of the meat mince, omit eggs and the rest of the recipe remains the same.

Serves 4
Preparation skill level: Difficult

For assembling

- Grease a casserole dish or a lasagne pan. Sprinkle breadcrumbs on the bottom. Place a layer of potatoes on the bottom. Top with a layer of eggplant slices.
- Put a layer of meat sauce on top of eggplant layer and sprinkle with ¼ of the grated cheese. Repeat layering the same way with meat sauce followed by eggplant and then cheese.
- Pour the béchamel sauce over the layered eggplant and allow sauce to fill the sides and corners of the pan. Smoothen the béchamel sauce surface and sprinkle with remaining grated cheese. Bake in a pre-heated oven at 180˚C or 350˚F, for 45 minutes or until the cheese melts and is golden in colour.

Ananya's Twist:

- Instead of covering the moussaka with béchamel sauce, a good variation could be to make a mixture of freshly grated Parmesan cheese and fresh breadcrumbs, and use this mixture to cover.
- Sliced and sautéed zucchini can be used instead of eggplants, and layered similarly in accordance with the recipe given.

Scandinavian Countries

DENMARK

Who has not heard of Danish or Danish pastry which is famous the world over. Danes are very proud of their cured fish, like herring or salmon, and whole grain rye bread. In view of long cold months in Denmark, food preservation techniques like curing and pickling have been practiced. Of late, Nordic food revolution has given the old techniques of preservations a modern twist by introducing fresh meat and vegetables.

Danish Pastry

A light flaky pastry filled with custard. In Denmark, it is called *Wiener Brod* or bread from Vienna.

2 cups or 300 gms all-purpose flour, plus extra for rolling

1⅓ cups or 225 gms cold unsalted butter, cut into small cubes

1 tsp sugar

1½ tsp dry yeast

⅓ cup lukewarm water

⅓ cup all-purpose flour

⅓ cup cold milk

2 egg yolks

¼ cup cold double cream

2½ tbsp castor sugar

1 tsp salt

1 cup prepared thin vanilla custard

½ cup dark raisins

1 egg, beaten for egg wash over the pastry

- Dissolve 1 teaspoon sugar in lukewarm water, stir in the yeast, add 50 grams flour until smooth, cover and leave it for 15 minutes to bubble.
- Add the milk, egg yolks, cream and sugar into the yeast mixture. Add the butter, flour and salt. Mix everything together to form a lumpy dough. Scrape the dough out on a floured work platform and roll the dough out to 1 cm thick rectangle. Fold it in by thirds (folding one-third of the rectangle first, and then fold over the other one third remaining). Roll it out again as before. Repeat the one-third fold-in process. Then wrap and chill for 30 minutes. Repeat this rolling and chilling sequence twice more. Then roll and shape as needed.

Tip: if using readymade puff pastry, then above two steps should be omitted.

- Roll out 30 cm (12 inch) x 15 cm (6 inch) with 1 cm thick rectangle from the dough. Spread a thin layer of custard and generously dot with plump, dark raisins. Roll tightly up along one side till the end to form a cylinder. Seal the edges with water. Cut 2 inches thick roundels from the cylinder. Flip them on baking tray to look like pinwheels.

Makes 8-10 Danish pastries
Preparation skill level: Difficult

- Leave the pinwheel shaped dough to rise in a warm place until almost doubled in size. Once risen, brush with beaten egg and bake at a pre-heated oven at 200˚C or 400˚F for 10 minutes, then at 180°C for another 15-20 minutes, until puffed up, flaky and golden brown.

NORWAY

Norwegian smoked salmon has been a significant contribution of Norway to the culinary world. *Gravlaks*, known elsewhere as dill-salmon is a popular salmon variant of curing in salt-sugar-dill leave solutions over several days. Due to its extreme cold climatic conditions, food preservation has been part and parcel of the cuisine, mainly through curing of meat and fish, and pickling of vegetables. Norwegians are known to celebrate big occasions through lively mixture of song and dance. What best could be served on such occasions, but *Verdens Beste*-World's Best Cake.

Verdens Beste Kvæfjordkake (World's Best Cake)

The national cake of Norway. A layered celebration cake.

For the cake

1 cup or 150 gms flour, sieved

¾ cup or 125 gms softened butter

½ cup or 75 gms powdered sugar

4 egg yolks (save the whites for the meringue)

2 tsp baking powder, sieved with the flour

4-6 tbsp milk

For the meringue

4 egg whites

1 tsp vinegar or lemon juice

1 cup or 150 gms powdered sugar

½ cup almonds, sliced fine (alternatively, you could use hazelnuts)

For the cake

- Beat the butter and sugar until light and fluffy. Add one egg yolk at a time, beating well after addition of each egg.
- Combine flour and the baking powder. Fold the flour and baking powder to the creamed butter and sugar, alternating with the milk, until a smooth cake batter is obtained. Using a spatula, spread batter into your prepared baking pan.

For the meringue

- Beat the egg whites and vinegar/lemon juice until almost stiff. Gradually add the sugar, and continue beating till the egg whites turn very stiff and meringue-like. (Tip: In case a part of the egg yolk by chance gets into the egg-white, then just remove it or discard the white, as you will never be able make meringues.)
- Spread this over the cake batter layer and sprinkle with the chopped almonds. Pour it in a greased 13 x 9 inches rectangular pan.

For the filling

3 egg yolks

¼ cup sugar

2 tsp cornflour

1 cup whole milk

¼ cup double cream

1 tsp vanilla extract

Good to know

Cornflour cannot be used directly as it turns into lumps; it needs to be dissolved in any liquid, and formed into slurry, before using.

Serves 6
Preparation skill level: Moderately difficult

- Bake in a pre-heated oven at 180°C or 350°F for 40-45 minutes or till the cake layer is completely cooked and the meringue top is set and just starts turning golden brown.
- Cool the cake on a cooling rack. Remove once cooled, slice the cake in two, thus giving two halves with meringue on the top.

For the filling

- Whisk together the egg yolks well with sugar till fluffy and pale. Add the cornflour, mix well and keep aside.
- Bring the milk and cream to a boil
- Pour the milk-cream mixture to the egg yolk mixture whisking briskly. Add the vanilla extract.
- Put the mixture back on heat. Stir continuously till it's very thick.
- Chill in a refrigerator for further use.
- To assemble, spread the prepared filling mixture over the cake base. Top with the other cake, meringue side up.

SWEDEN

Sweden is known for its meatballs (or *kottbullar*), herrings and *Knäckebröd*. *Smörgåsbord*, the very famous Swedish-style buffet starting with a cold fish dish and moving on either to cold or hot dishes. Swedish meatballs are an essential part of a typical *Smörgåsbord*, and centred around different types of pickled-herring. *Knäckebröd*, the famed Swedish crisp-bread (substitute for fresh breads), baked and had for over hundreds of years, with a long shelf-life, was developed due to the cold climes of the country. It can be topped with almost anything, including boiled eggs, caviar or even plain butter; a very versatile bread indeed.

Swedish Meatballs

Meatballs, usually forming part of *Smörgåsbord*,
a type of Scandinavian meal, served buffet-style with multiple dishes.

½ cup or 75 gms lamb mince (traditionally made with half ground beef and half cup ground lean pork)
½ cup fine dry breadcrumbs
½ cup fresh cream
½ cup water
Salt to taste
½ tsp dried mixed herbs
2 tbsp minced garlic
¼ cup finely chopped onion
1 egg, beaten
3 tbsp butter

Vegetarian Option: Substitute the meat mince with soya mince and omit egg.

- Mix the breadcrumbs, cream and water. Keep aside for 5 minutes. (Tip: Soaking the breadcrumbs in cream and water results in super soft and moist meatballs)
- Mix the lamb mince, salt, herbs, garlic and onion. Then add the breadcrumbs-cream mixture. Add the egg. Mix and bind well.
- Shape into small balls. Heat butter in a pan. Add 10 to 15 meatballs. Fry over moderate heat until the meatballs are browned and cooked through.
- Served best with boiled potatoes, and tossed salad.

Makes 8-10 meatballs
Preparation skill level: Very easy

Hungary | Russia | Poland

Hungary has contributed *Goulash*, pronounced *'gulyas'*, to the world. It is synonymous with the country itself, deriving its main colour and flavour from paprika and lard (pork-fat). These are Hungarian cuisine's main ingredients, making the outcome very appetising, but also highly calorific.

Russians say bread is the beginning of everything - Russians love their bread. They have it in all shapes and colours – black bread, white bread, delicious Georgian bread, dome shaped bread, and so on. Russian cuisine is very colourful - as vibrant as their many festivals. *Bortsch*, a bright-red beetroot soup served with sour cream, providing a superb colour contrast. *Blini*, brown pancakes served with orange-coloured caviar and sour cream. To top it all, how can one speak of Russian cuisine without the mention of its national drink – the colourless *Vodka* served in numerous ways and concoctions?

The **Polish** love hearty meals – though it may add a few ounces to their midriffs, due to its richness. Sausages and bread form the most important part of Polish food. The delicious *Pierogi* (fried or steamed dumplings with assorted fillings) is Poland's most popular dish. They take pride in the variety of this exquisite preparation. The national dish however is *Bigos*, or hunter's stew, usually containing pork or sometimes rabbit, may not be everyone's delicacy but an acquired taste.

Hungarian Goulash

Slow cooked rustic stew made with lamb/beef/pork.

500 gms lamb or mutton, cubed
Salt and pepper to taste
2 tbsp flour
3 tbsp vegetable oil
1 large onion, finely chopped
1 green chilli, deseeded and chopped
2 carrots, peeled and chopped
1 stick celery, finely chopped

- Mix salt, pepper and ½ tsp mixed herbs to the flour. Coat the meat in the flour.
- Heat the oil in heavy bottomed pan. Fry the onion, chilli, carrot and celery. Add the meat and fry until browned.
- Add the paprika, tomato paste, nutmeg, rest of the mixed herbs, salt and pepper and cook for further 2 minutes. Add the stock, chopped tomatoes, red wine and Worcestershire sauce. Bring to a simmer.

1 tsp paprika

1 tbsp tomato paste

A pinch of grated nutmeg

3 tsp mixed herbs

¾ cup chicken stock

2 tomatoes, finely chopped

¾ cups red wine (optional)

3 tbsp Worcestershire sauce

- Transfer the contents to the slow cooker to cook for about 5 hours. Alternatively transfer the goulash to a deep oven-proof dish. Cover with aluminium foil and bake for about 3 hours in low temperature at 130°C or 250°F.

Ananya's Twist:

After step 3, transfer the contents of the goulash in a pressure cooker and cook till 6-7 whistles for a quicker result.

Vegetarian Option: Use large soya chunks instead of the meat.

Serves 4
Preparation skill level: Moderately easy

Blini

Pancakes made of buckwheat flour and yeast.
Served with melted butter, sour cream, and other garnishes such as caviar.
Popular in Russia, Poland, Ukraine and other eastern European countries.

1½ cups buckwheat flour
(Alternative: use all-purpose flour)

Salt to taste

1 tsp rapid-rise yeast

1 tsp sugar

1 cup lukewarm milk

2 tbsp melted butter

1 egg, separated

Serves 6
Preparation skill level: Easy

- Add salt to the buckwheat flour. Make a well in the centre. Add yeast, sugar and milk. Mix well. Cover and let the batter rise until doubled in size. This process will take about 1 hour.
- Add the melted butter and egg yolk into batter. Whisk the egg white until stiff and fold into the batter. Keep aside for 15 minutes.
- Heat a pan. Pour about ¼ cup of batter without spreading. Bubbles will form on the surface of the blini. Cook for about 1 minute on one side before turning it over. Repeat with remaining batter.
- Served best with various toppings like caviar, smoked salmon, boiled eggs, sour cream, chopped dill-leaves, pitted olives and lemon wedges.

Good to know

- To make sour cream: If sour cream is difficult to obtain, you can make it by adding 1 teaspoon lemon juice to ⅔ cup of single cream; stir well and leave to thicken. Sour cream is ready.
- 'Blini' is happiness: Blini is compared to the sun, symbolising rich harvests and happy marriages.
- Caviar, the king of eggs:
  - The ultimate treat: While caviar is a mouthful of fish eggs or roe, but for some it's an ultimate gourmet experience. The most expensive and prized caviar is 'beluga'.
  - Symbol of luxury and prosperity: Caviar is Russia's most well-known culinary treat. In the olden days, a person's status was determined by the quantum of caviar served.

Pierogi

Dumplings with a variety of savoury fillings.

For the filling

2 cups boiled and mashed potato

2 tbsp butter/olive oil

1 cup finely chopped onions

1 cup grated Cheddar cheese

Salt and pepper to taste

For the dough

2 cups all-purpose flour

¼ cup melted butter

1 cup warm water

Ananya's Twist:

Add chopped green chillies or red pepper flakes to the potato mixture for a spicy kick.

Makes 12-15 pierogi
Preparation skill level: Moderately difficult

For the filling

- Heat butter in a pan. Add the onions and fry till golden-brown and soft. The process will take about 15-20 minutes. Reserve half of the onions for garnish and add the other half to the mashed potatoes. Add the cheese, 1 teaspoon salt, and ½ teaspoon pepper and mix until well combined. Let it cool down to room temperature before using.

For the dough

- Knead dough using flour, butter and warm water until soft and pliable. Cover with a wet kitchen towel.
- Divide the dough into 6 orange-size balls. Working with 1 piece of dough at a time on a floured work surface, and keeping the others covered enables the dough to remain soft and not dry out. Roll the dough into a thin circle of 12 inch diameter.
- Using a floured 3 inch round cookie cutter, cut out circles of dough. Taking one dough circle at a time, spoon 1 tablespoon of the prepared filling into the centre of the circle and fold it in half. Press and seal the edges. Arrange the filled pierogi in a line leaving space between each other. Repeat with the remaining dough circles and filling.
- Drop the pierogi into the boiling water and give them a gentle stir so they don't stick together. When they float to the top (after 1 to 2 minutes), take them out with a slotted spoon.
- Sprinkle the pierogi with the reserved onion, and serve with the sour cream on the side.

Serving suggestions:

- Pierogi can either be boiled (as stated above) or fried.
    - For boiled pierogi, melt the butter and sprinkle on top of pierogi with the reserved onion and drizzle with melted butter. Serve hot with the sour cream on the side.
    - For fried pierogi, melt 4 tablespoons of the butter in a pan, cook the boiled pierogi, flipping once, until golden-brown and crusty on both sides.
- Filling can be altered. You can use meat or chicken or other vegetables instead of potato and cheese.

Russian Bortsch

Thick beetroot soup served with sour cream.

2 large beet roots, peeled and boiled and grated

2 tbsp oil

½ cup onion, grated

1 cup carrot, grated

2 large potatoes, chopped

1 cup shredded cabbage

1 cup of vegetable stock (chicken stock can also be used)

1 tbsp lemon juice

2 bay leaves

3 tbsp tomato ketchup

1 cup of any boiled white beans

Salt and pepper to taste

A dollop of sour cream

Dill leaves to garnish

- Heat oil. Sauté the onions and carrots. Cook till tender.
- Add the potatoes, cabbage and the grated beetroot to the onion-carrot mixture. Add chicken/vegetable stock, lemon juice, bay leaves, tomato ketchup and boiled beans. Season with salt and pepper and cook for 12-15 minutes on low heat till cabbage is tender.
- Blend everything in a food processor.
- Serve with a dollop of sour cream and a sprig of dill leaves.

Good to know

- Ordinary can be extra-ordinary: An amazing simple recipe from just a few mundane ingredients like beets, cabbage, potatoes, and tomato paste. It provides a hearty warm soup, to combat the harsh wintry climes of the region.

Serves 4
Preparation skill level: Easy

ROMANIA

Rich in natural resources, Romania has been invaded for over centuries. No wonder the Romanian cuisine has been influenced by Greek, Byzantine, Arab and the Armenians. Romania has been under occupation from Turks, Hungarians, Austrians, Poles, Bulgaria and Russians. The locals have thus learnt to eat on the run, being under constant threat. This led to consumption of raw herbs, salads and vegetables, dry and cured raw meat. Post Ottoman-era, and against the Islamic influence, the Romanians wanted to make themselves self-sufficient. This led to corn cultivation and pig-farming. Abundance of corn and use of *polenta* (a corn-meal) gave rise to the famous mamaliga dishes in its cuisine. Pork is the most preferred choice of meat.

Romanian Mamaliga Balls

Polenta balls stuffed with salami. A popular Romanian snack.

2 cups fine yellow cornmeal

1 cup salami, roughly chopped (may add finely chopped onion and grated cheese to the salami mixture to make it spicy)

1 tbsp butter

2½ cups water

¾ teaspoon salt

Vegetarian Option: Prepare the fillings with finely chopped spring onions and grated Cheddar cheese.

Makes 6-8 mamaliga balls
Preparation skill level: Moderately easy

- Mix cornmeal, butter, water and salt in a pan. Bring to a boil, stirring continuously till thick. Stir in butter and adjust seasonings. Cool slightly.
- Using a cookie scoop, portion out balls while still warm. Flatten mamaliga or the prepared polenta mixture in the palm of your hand, add spoonful of salami in the middle. Seal completely and roll into a ball.
- Fry balls for 2-3 minutes or until golden brown. Drain on paper towels.
- Served best warm with fresh herbs and marinara dipping sauce.

Ananya's Twist:

- Add finely chopped onions and chillies to the salami mixture to give an extra kick.
- After stuffing the mamaliga balls, instead of frying, keep it aside. Prepare a sauce with tomatoes, tomato ketchup, garlic and olive oil. Season the sauce with salt and pepper and bring it to a boil. Add the prepared balls to the sauce and cook till well coated. This will give a different tangy taste.

AFRICA

African cuisine is a mix of cultures, colonialism, trade routes and history spiced with traditional fruits and vegetables, exotic game meat and fish from the ocean. It would be impossible to categorise any one country's cuisine as African cuisine. Every country in this vast continent has diverse eating habits. Culinary experiences will vastly differ from food served while on a safari in Kenya, from eating at the French and British influenced restaurants of Johannesburg in South Africa. The variety extends from tasting of *Doro Wat* of Ethiopia, Nigerian *Jollof Rice*, the coconut and fish stews of Nairobi, or *Tagines* from Morocco, to the Muslim dominated North African Egyptian dish like *Kusharis* (a concoction of rice, noodles and pasta). All of these and many more together make up African cuisine.

NIGERIA

The name Nigeria is taken from the Niger River, which plays an important part in Nigerian lives. Not only is it a transportation highway, it is an excellent source of fish, including carp, Nile-perch and catfish. Nigeria is one of the world's most ethnically diverse countries. With its varied cultures, it is difficult to pick one national dish. Soups, stews and dishes using yam are extremely popular. *Jollof rice* is eaten by all and is part of celebration menus.

Jollof Rice

Spicy tomato rice – popular at parties and family get-togethers.

1 cup long grain Nigerian rice (Substitute: Basmati rice)
2 tbsp tomato purée
2 tbsp tomato ketchup
4 tbsp oil
1 cup onions, sliced
½ cup capsicum, sliced
1 tsp red pepper flakes
2 tbsp garlic, minced
1 tsp chilli powder
1 tsp ground cumin
1 tsp paprika
Salt and pepper to taste
1 stock cube (vegetarian)
2 cups water
Handful of chopped parsley or coriander leaves

Good to know

Basmati rice: In case using Basmati rice, soak for 20 minutes. Soaking in water enables the rice to be eventually fluffy and long while cooking, but care should be taken not to over soak as the rice might break while cooking.

- Rinse the rice well.
- Heat oil in a pan. Add onions, capsicum and red pepper flakes and minced garlic. Sauté well. Stir in the chilli powder, cumin, paprika, and pepper. Cook for 2-3 minutes. Crumble the stock cube and mix well and cook for 2 minutes.
- Mix tomato purée, tomato ketchup, and water.
- Bring to a boil and stir in the soaked rice. Cook covered for 15 minutes.
- Leave to stand for 10 minutes, lid on, before serving.
- Garnish with chopped parsley or coriander leaves.

Serves 3-4
Preparation skill level: Easy

MOROCCO

In Morocco, having meals is a social ritual. A host might take up to a week to prepare a suitable dinner for guests. A typical meal will often consist of as many as fifty courses. Desert nomads have influenced the Moroccan diet, using mutton, vegetables and dairy produce. There is also a significant Arabic influence. Over the centuries the cuisine has incorporated European, sub-Saharan, African and Spanish eating patterns. *B'stilla* (a crisp pastry, rolled as thin as a tissue paper, filled with chicken; which is a full day's work to make) and *Brochette* (kebabs flavoured with bits of beef or lamb fat) are extremely popular. Another Moroccan speciality is the vessel *Tajine*, in which chicken or meat in spicy stew is simmered for hours. The purist Moroccan preparations are however slowly being influenced by modernity – it will not be surprising to find pressure-cookers being used to make the legendary *tagine*.

Chicken Tagine with Preserved Lemons

Tagine means a cooking vessel. Chicken tagine is a fragrant dish, and is traditionally made in a special cooking vessel.

1 skinless chicken, cut into 8 pieces

1 preserved lemon, quartered and seeds removed (usage of preserved lemon is unique to Moroccan cookery) [Recipe provided]

2 onions, chopped

2 tbsp garlic, minced

2 tsp ginger, minced

1 tsp ground pepper

1 tsp turmeric

Handful of fresh chopped coriander leaves

Handful of fresh chopped parsley

¼ tsp saffron threads, crumbled (optional)

4 tsp smen (Moroccan homemade butter) (Possible substitute: Ghee or clarified butter)

- Blend onion, garlic, ginger, pepper, turmeric, coriander, parsley and half of the preserved lemon in a blender. Pulse to make a coarse paste. Mix the prepared paste with chicken, add saffron the remaining chopped preserved lemon flesh and smen/ghee and let it marinate for few hours.
- Pour most of the olive oil into the tagine vessel, and spread it to the bottom of the vessel.

  (Substitute for tagine vessel: If tagine vessel is unavailable, use a heavy bottomed pan and use a tight lid to retain the steam and slow cook.)
- Arrange the chicken pieces side by side at the bottom of the tagine. Sprinkle with salt and scatter the marinated mixture all around.
- Place the olives and preserved lemon quarters, and drizzle the remaining olive oil over the chicken.
- Add water to the tagine, cover, and place on a diffuser over a medium-low heat.

1 handful of olives

⅓ cup olive oil

Salt to taste

¼ cup water

Recipe for Preserved Lemon

4 medium lemon, cut into quarters

½ cup salt

1 tbsp black pepper

- Simmer for 45 minutes till the chicken is tender. Let the tagine cool down a bit before serving.

Serves 4
Preparation skill level: Moderately easy

- Layer the lemon in a glass jar. As you layer the lemons, use spoonfuls of salt, and press the lemon to release their juices. Seal the jar. Refrigerate for 2-3 weeks.
- The jar should be shaken daily, so that the lemons and juices mix properly.
- The salt transforms the lemon rind, mellows the flavour and softens the texture of the lemon. The preserved lemon is ready and can be used in various dishes.

Piri-Piri Prawns with Harissa Couscous

Spicy couscous with chilli-prawns. Piri-piri is the African word for bird's-eye chilli; harissa is an African chilli paste; and couscous is a staple in North Africa.

For the piri-piri prawns

12 large prawns, cleaned, deveined and shelled, but tails left on

2 fresh red chillies, roughly chopped

1 dried chilli, roughly chopped

1 tsp lemon juice

3 cloves of garlic

1 tbsp smoked paprika

1 tbsp red wine vinegar

Salt and pepper to taste

4 tbsp olive oil

For the couscous

1⅓ cups couscous

1 tsp harissa (chilli paste from Africa, available in bottles at gourmet supermarkets)

1 tbsp pomegranate molasses (pomegranate juice cooked until it becomes thick; used in African and middle eastern cookery)

1⅓ cups boiling water

1 tsp lemon juice

1 red onion, finely sliced

½ cup pomegranate kernels

Coriander leaves, as required

1 lemon for garnishing

Salt and pepper to taste

Vegetarian Option: Harissa couscous is vegetarian and can be a dish on its own. The prawns can be substituted with paneer or cottage cheese cubes.

For the piri-piri prawns

- Blend all the ingredients except the prawns in a food processor until smooth. This paste makes the piri-piri sauce.
- Marinate the prawns in prepared sauce and refrigerate for an hour.
- Cook the prawns for 2 minutes on each side in a hot pan, or until the prawns turns pink and are cooked through.

For the couscous

- Pour boiling water over couscous in a large bowl. Stir well with a fork to combine. Add the harissa, pomegranate molasses, lemon juice, season with salt and pepper, and mix well. Cover with cling film and set aside until the couscous absorbs all the liquid and swells.
- Add the red onion, pomegranate kernels and coriander leaves. Mix well.
- Serve the piri-piri prawns over a bed of prepared harrissa-couscous garnished with lemon.

Tip: If you don't want your chillies to be very hot, you can reduce the heat by taking out the seeds. The spice factor in chillies lies in the pip where the seeds are attached. By discarding the pip and seeds, the chilli can be used liberally. It will only add to the chilli flavour.

Good to know

Bland but made delicious: Couscous is light fluffy textured yellow grain, made from semolina. Its bland flavour makes it a perfect accompaniment with the rich sauces or North African cuisine.

Pre-cooked couscous: In olden times, it took a long time to steam and prepare couscous. But nowadays, the pre-cooked couscous is readily available and requires only soaking in boiling water. However it will need steaming for 10 minutes if it is not of the pre-cooked variety; please check the instruction on the packet.

Serves 3-4

Preparation skill level: Moderately easy

ETHIOPIA

It is lovely to have a hearty meal in *Ethiopia*. It provides a feeling of bonhomie - guests eat from one platter. Diners sit around large spongy-flat bread – locally known as *injera*. Meals are served on this large platter. Various dishes are portioned out onto *injera*, and diners simply tear off a piece of the bread (without forks and spoons), use it to scoop up some of the various *wats* (stews) and pop it in their mouth. Most of the preparations use *berberé* (pronounced bear-bear-ee), a spicy red pepper paste. Unlike most African countries, Ethiopia has remained somewhat isolated with its mountainous geography, not being influenced by the Europeans (except for a very brief spell of Italian occupation under Mussolini). However, due to it being on the ancient trade routes, Ethiopia cuisine makes creative use of spices like cardamom, cloves, cinnamon, and fenugreek.

Injera Bread

Ethiopian sour dough crêpe. This is used as daily-staple bread, with its spongy texture helping to soak up the meat or vegetable gravy.

2 cups all-purpose flour
½ cup whole wheat flour
½ cup cornmeal
1 tbsp baking powder
1 tsp active dry yeast
½ tsp salt
3 cups lukewarm water
2 cups club soda
2 tbsp lemon juice

Makes 8 injera breads
Preparation skill level: Moderately easy

- Mix the flour, whole wheat flour, cornmeal, baking powder and yeast in a bowl. Season with salt. Add 3 cups of lukewarm water and mix well to form a consistency of a thick pancake batter. Cover and keep it aside for two days till batter is fermented.
- Just before preparing the injera, add the club soda to the batter. Mix well till frothy.
- Heat a non-stick skillet (i.e. pan). Ladle about ½ cup of the batter on it and spread it with a spatula to make a large crêpe. Cook till all the bubbles are formed on top, about 2-3 minutes on each side.
- Cook the rest of the batter using the same method.
- Brush each injera with the lemon juice.
- Served best piping hot.

Good to know

Tough to get 'teff': Traditionally Injera is made with teff (poppy-seed sized fine-grain) flour which is unavailable in most countries. This recipe with all-purpose flour works well and is a close substitute.

Doro Wat

Slow-cooked Ethiopian chicken stew with spicy berberé paste.

4 pieces each of chicken drumsticks and thighs

½ cup berberé paste (spice mixture which serves as a key ingredient in the cuisines of Ethiopia. Recipe follows)

1 tbsp lemon juice

Salt and pepper to taste

1 cup chopped onions

1 tbsp garlic, minced

1 tbsp ginger, minced

2 tbsp paprika

¼ cup oil

¼ cup butter or niter kibbeh (homemade African butter); (Possible substitute: Ghee or clarified butter)

½ cup water or stock

¼ cup red wine (Substitute: Red wine vinegar or malt vinegar)

4 hard-boiled eggs

- Marinate the chicken pieces in lemon juice and salt for half hour.
- Purée the onions, garlic and ginger. Heat the oil and butter in a large pan. Add the paprika to colour the oil. Stir in the berberé paste and cook for 2 to 3 minutes. Add the onion-garlic-ginger purée and sauté until cooked well and oil leaves the sides of the paste. Add the water or stock and wine and stir-in the chicken pieces. Add salt and pepper to taste. Bring to a boil. Cover and simmer for 25 minutes.
- Add the whole hard boiled eggs and cook for another 10 to 15 minutes, or until the chicken is very tender.
- Served best with injera bread.

Vegetarian Option: The stew can be made with soya chunks instead of the chicken.

Serves 4
Preparation skill level: Difficult

Berberé Paste

1 tsp each of cumin, turmeric, red pepper flakes, cardamom, fenugreek seeds, peppercorn, cloves and allspice (African/Jamaican spice mix)

1 cup onion, chopped

1 tbsp each of minced ginger, minced garlic, and paprika

2-3 dried red chillies

A pinch of nutmeg

½ cup oil

1 cup water or red wine

Salt to taste

- Dry roast all the dry spices. Then grind everything in a food processor. This paste can be used in most of Ethiopian cooking.

SOUTH AFRICA

South African cuisine perhaps has one of the most profound influences of several cultures over the years. The Dutch, Germans, French, English and Malays (who were brought in as slaves by the Dutch from South East Asia), have all left their imprints on South African cuisine. With God's gift of ample quantities of great seafood, plentiful wild-game, marvellous lamb, numerous varieties of fruits and vegetables, the South Africans have a large repertoire to choose from. However, rice, potatoes and meat remain the cornerstone of its cooking ingredients. The blending of East with West, a variation of European fish and meat, spiced with mostly Indian spices and often sweetened. *Bobotie* (a dish with Cape Malay origin), the South African national dish, captures this essence.

Bobotie

Meat and egg baked dish—a cross between a meat loaf and shepherd's pie.

500 gms lamb mince
3 eggs
Oil as required
1 tbsp garlic, minced
2 onions, chopped
1 chilli, finely chopped
1 tbsp curry powder
1 thick slice of white bread, crust removed
½ cups milk
1 tbsp vinegar
1 tbsp lemon juice
1 tsp brown sugar
Salt to taste
1 tbsp mango chutney
1 tbsp apricot jam/preserve
A handful of raisins
6 bay leaves

Serves 3-4
Preparation skill level: Moderate

- Heat oil in a pan. Add the garlic, onion, chilli and curry powder. Sauté well for 2 minutes, add minced meat. Fry until the meat is almost done.
- Soak the bread in milk for 15-20 minutes. Squeeze out the bread and keep the remaining milk aside.
- Add the squeezed bread, vinegar, lemon juice, sugar, salt and chutney, jam and raisins to the mince. Sauté for 1 minutes and keep aside.
- Take a flat baking dish or a pie dish and place three bay leaves at the bottom. Place the prepared mince mixture into the dish.
- Beat the eggs in the remaining milk, and pour over the mince. Place 3 bay leaves on top of dish. Place the dish in a pre-heated oven and cook for 30 minutes at 170°C or 325°F. Served best with plain green salad, chutney and yellow rice.

Vegetarian Option: Substitute the meat mince with soya granules and omit eggs.

Ananya's Twist:

Instead of lamb or beef mince, chicken mince can be used. But the cooking time of chicken is lesser. Hence, sautéing of chicken in a pan or pre-cooking is not required. It can be directly used with all other ingredients.

SOUTH EAST ASIA

Simplicity is the corner-stone for South East Asian cuisine. A bowl of rice or noodles describes this simplicity the best. Stretching over a vast area, from Indonesia to Myanmar, including Malaysia, Thailand, Vietnam, Laos, Cambodia, Philippines, Singapore, it is varied and diverse. Hong Kong, though debatable whether it should form part of culinary-map of China or not, can also be included in this region given its style of cooking. A speciality of the South-East Asian cuisine is the use of lime leaves, lemon grass and galangal – which are not used in any other cuisine in the world. Though simple to look at, the cooking medium and methods could be rich and complex, and often difficult to replicate.

THAILAND

Equilibrium, detail and variety, play an important role in Thai cuisine. Thai food is essentially a balance of the five fundamental taste, namely: hot (spicy), sour, sweet, salty, and bitter. Thai cuisine emphasises light meals with strong aromatic overtones and high spice factor. Thai people with their Buddhist background shunned the use of meat in large chunks. Meat is thus normally finely shredded and laced with herbs and spices. Many of the fresh herbs and spices used in Thai cooking are galangal, lemongrass, fresh bird's-eye chillies, kaffir lime and lime leaves. Another speciality of Thai food is their fruit and vegetable carvings. These have fascinated and mesmerised the world with its intricate details.

Som Tam

A delicious tangy raw papaya salad.

2 cups shredded green papaya
1 clove garlic
2 bird's-eye chillies
1 tbsp dried shrimp (dried fish has a strong odour, and is an acquired taste. Omit if found very strong.)
2 tbsp toasted peanuts
1½ tbsp fish sauce
2 tbsp lime juice
6 cherry tomatoes
6 French beans
1½ tbsp palm sugar
(Possible substitute: Brown sugar)

Vegetarian Option: For a vegetarian *som tam*, omit the dried shrimp and substitute soy sauce for fish sauce.

Serves 3-4
Preparation skill level: Easy

- In a mortar and pestle, grind together garlic, chillies, dried shrimp (if using), toasted peanuts, fish sauce, lime juice and palm sugar to form a coarse paste. Then add French beans and halved cherry tomatoes. Pound a few times to bruise the beans and get the juice out of the tomatoes. Mix the shredded papaya well with the dressing.
- Serve with sticky rice and a sliver of cabbage, French beans and Thai basil.

Pad Thai

Thai style, stir-fried flat noodles, one of the most popular street foods.

1 packet dried flat rice noodles (equivalent to 2 cups when boiled)

3 tbsp fish sauce (some people find the smell of fish sauce a bit strong. It can be substituted with light soy sauce. But authenticity is lost.)

Warm water as required

3 tbsp tamarind paste

1 tbsp palm sugar

2 tbsp oyster sauce

1½ tbsp Thai hot chilli sauce

½ cup chicken stock

½ cup vegetable oil

1 tbsp chopped garlic

7-8 medium shrimp, peeled and develned

1 cup chicken breast, cut into thin strips

2 eggs, beaten

1 cup bean sprouts

3-4 spring onions, chopped into 2 inch pieces

2 tbsp chopped unsalted dry-roasted peanuts

¼ cup chopped fresh coriander leaves

Few lime wedges to garnish

Serves 3-4
Preparation skill level: Moderately easy

- Soak the noodles for 10 minutes in warm water.
- Mix together the fish sauce, if using, tamarind paste, sugar, oyster sauce, chilli sauce with the chicken stock. Set aside.
- Heat 3 teaspoons oil in a wok. Stir in garlic, then add the shrimp and chicken; cook, stirring constantly until shrimp is opaque and chicken is cooked through for 2-3 minutes Keep aside.
- Heat 2 teaspoons oil in the same pan. Pour the eggs in the centre. Stir and cook the eggs till firm. Keep aside.
- Add the remaining oil in the pan. Add the noodles to the wok and mix the prepared sauce. Cook the noodles till soft. Add the reserved eggs, shrimp and chicken and mix well. Add bean sprouts and spring onions. Mix and take it off the fire.
- Add the crushed roasted peanuts and serve garnished with fresh coriander and lime wedges on the side.

Vegetarian option: Replace the chicken, prawns and eggs with veggies like carrots, beans, mushrooms, and broccoli. Replace the fish sauce with soy sauce and use a vegetarian oyster sauce. Use vegetable stock instead of chicken stock.

Good to know

- All time eats: A noodle dish, had for breakfast, lunch and dinner, in the streets of Thai cities.

Some South-East Asian ingredients which may not be palatable all though popular with the locals:

- Shrimp paste: It has a very strong odour and taste; used as a seasoning rather than an independent ingredient.
- Fish sauce (*nam pla*): It is used substituting salt in many cuisines; has a strong odour.

Tom Yum Goong

Extremely popular spicy prawn ('goong' means prawns) clear soup.

7-8 medium shrimp, peeled and deveined (keep the shrimp head aside for making stock)

2 cups water

1 lemon grass, finely chopped (Tip: Use the lemon grass heart only. Discard the woody bits)

2-3 kaffir lime leaves

4 slices galangal (similar to ginger but more pungent) (Substitute: If unavailable, ginger, but not an equivalent substitute)

4 bird's-eye chillies (these chillies are special from Thailand, extremely hot; but renders special flavours for which Thailand is famous for) (Substitute: If unavailable, locally grown small variety of red-chillies)

1½ tbsp fish sauce (fish sauce is the salt component for all South East Asian counties)

1 tbsp lemon juice

1 tsp palm-sugar (Substitute: Brown sugar)

1 tsp hot chilli-paste (can be obtained from Asian supermarkets or groceries)

1 tbsp tom yum soup paste (Optional; can be obtained from Asian supermarkets)

4 button mushrooms, halved

Coriander leaves, for garnishing

- Add the shrimp heads and shells to 2 cups of water and cook for 20 minutes. Discard the shells and drain the stock.
- Cook the stock along with chopped lemon grass, kaffir lime leaves, galangal, bird's-eye chillies, fish sauce, lemon juice, sugar, and chilli paste and tom-yum paste. Boil for 5 minutes, add shrimps and mushrooms. Cook for further 3 minutes. Garnish with coriander leaves.

Vegetarian option: Start with vegetable stock. Replace the shrimp with veggies like carrots, beans, baby corn and mushrooms. Replace fish sauce with soy sauce.

Good to know

Therapeutic yummy Tom-Yum: Research reports say that a 'Tom-Yum a day keeps cancer at bay'. The ingredients such as galangal, kaffir lime leaves, and lemon grass, are rich anti-oxidants.

Serves 3-4
Preparation skill level: Easy

Kaeng Khiao Wan Gai

Green chicken curry is one of the most popular Thai dishes savoured all across the globe.

250 gms boneless chicken thighs cut into cubes (Possible variation: Fish, vegetables, or paneer)

2 tbsp fresh green curry paste (Recipe follows; however, readymade green curry pastes can be used as it is readily available in supermarkets)

2 tbsp oil

4-5 kaffir lime leaves

1 cup mixed vegetables, like broccoli, cauliflower, zucchini

½ cup Thai eggplants (Possible substitute: Regular diced eggplants)

2 cups fresh coconut milk (Possible substitute: Canned coconut milk or coconut milk powder dissolved in water)

½ cup water

2-3 tbsp fish sauce (Fish sauce is a liquid, extracted from the fermentation of fish with sea salt. It is a salt substitute for South-East Asian cooking. It is one of the key ingredient for Thai cooking.)

2 tsp soy sauce

2 tsp palm sugar, powdered

2 tsp lime juice

- Heat oil in a pan. Add the green curry paste till it emits a nice aroma.
- Add the kaffir lime leaves, vegetables, and stir-fry for 3-4 minutes.
- Add coconut milk, and add some water to adjust consistency.
- Cook for 5 minutes. Add the chicken cubes and the fish sauce, (fish sauce is extremely salty. Hence addition of salt is not required) cook for 2-3 minutes.
- Add soy sauce and palm sugar followed by lime juice. Curry is ready. Served best with hot steamed rice.

To make coconut milk: Grate one coconut and blend it along with ½ cup of warm water, for 2-3 minutes. Pass this mixture through a sieve. The extract collected is the freshly made thick coconut milk.

Tip: Using fresh coconut milk and making a fresh curry paste for this recipe, converts the preparation from being an easy recipe to a difficult one, but the result will be worth taking the trouble.

Good to know

- All about coconut milk: If any recipe calls for 'thin' coconut milk, then the remnants of the coconut after extracting the 'thick' milk can be blended with warm water and sieved again.

Vegetarian option: Prepare the vegetarian curry paste with the given recipe. Replace chicken with broccoli, zucchini and baby corn.

Serves 3-4

Preparation skill level: Very easy if using the ready to use curry paste and coconut milk. If making it from scratch, it is difficult but rewarding in taste.

Fresh green curry paste

1 tbsp coriander roots

3-4 kaffir lime leaves

Handful of Thai basil

5 green bird's-eye chilli (with increase or decrease of chillies, the spice factor can be adjusted)

2 tsp coriander seeds

½ tsp peppercorns

1 tsp cumin

3 tbsp sliced shallots

1 tbsp sliced lemongrass

1 tsp shredded galangal

Salt to taste

1 tbsp minced garlic

1 teaspoon shrimp paste (optional as it may be found to be strong)

- Toast coriander seeds, peppercorns and cumin in a pan until light brown.
- Slice shallots, lemongrass, galangal, and coriander roots, into small pieces.
- Using a mortar and a pestle, grind the spices into powder. Add lemongrass and galangal into the mortar. Grind them. Add salt, garlic, kaffir lime leaves, coriander roots, Thai basil and shrimp paste (if using). Add fresh green chillies and leaves next. Pound until the mixture turns into a fine paste. Takes about 15 minutes.

VIETNAM

Vietnamese food is claimed to be one of the healthiest in the world, with emphasis on rice, wheat and legumes, abundance of fresh herbs and vegetables, fragrant with lemon grass, mint and basil, minimal use of oil, and treatment of meat as a condiment rather than a main course. Westerners love Vietnamese cuisine as it's more often sweet than spicy, though chillies are used. The Vietnamese chefs call their cuisine as *'The Nouvelle cuisine of Asia'* (the new-age French cooking). The cuisine reflects the influence of French, Chinese, Mongolian and Cambodian colonisation. Vietnamese love their noodles – the basic food consumed almost three times daily by the common man.

Pho Noodle Soup

A classic Vietnamese noodle soup with an aromatic broth garnished with meat and vegetables.

½ packet or 250 gms rice noodles
1 cup lean beef sirloin (Substitute for beef: Lamb or chicken or pork)
Hot water, as required
Oil, as required
1 large onion, cut into thick slices
1 tbsp ginger slices
3 cups chicken stock
3 cups water
5 star anise pods
1 (2 inch) cinnamon stick
2-4 tbsp fish sauce
Salt and pepper to taste
4 spring onions, thinly sliced
½ cup fresh coriander leaves, chopped
1 cup fresh bean sprouts
2 jalapeno chillies, finely chopped
2 bird's-eye chilli, finely chopped

- Soak rice noodles in hot water for 10 minutes. Drain and keep aside.
- Heat oil in a pan. Add the onion and ginger and cook about 4 minutes. Add the stock, 3 cups water, the star anise and cinnamon and simmer 20 minutes. Add the fish sauce to the stock and boil 5 minutes. Discard the ginger, star anise and cinnamon stick.
- Pierce the meat all over with a fork and season with salt and pepper. Sear the meat on a griddle pan until charred 2 to 3 minutes per side, and then transfer to a plate and rest. Thinly slice the meat against the grain.
- Divide the prepared noodles among 4 bowls; top with the prepared broth, meat slices, spring onions, coriander leaves, bean sprouts, jalapenos, chillies and onion.

Good to know

'Pho' literally means your own bowl. No two bowls of this soup are the same. It is the aromatic broth, which is the common element. Variation arises in its toppings – some prefer hoisin sauce, some chillies and fish-sauce, some have it with a squeeze of lime, and the possibilities are unending.

Vegetarian Option: Use strips of firm tofu instead of the meat.

Serves 3-4
Preparation skill level: Moderately easy

Rice Paper Rolls

Fresh salads, noodles, prawns, chicken, rolled in rice paper and served with a dipping sauce.

10-12 round rice paper sheets (6 inch diameter)

20-25 medium shrimp, peeled and deveined and blanched

1 cup chicken breast, boiled and cut into strips

2 cups cooked rice vermicelli noodles

1 small head of iceberg lettuce, washed and torn into strips

1 cup fresh mint leaves

1 cup fresh Thai basil leaves

1 cup fresh coriander leaves

1 medium cucumber, peeled, deseeded and cut into matchsticks

For the dipping sauce

2 small, red bird's-eye chillies, cut into fine slices

1 garlic clove, minced

1 tbsp palm sugar

2 tbsp lime juice

¼ cup fish sauce

1 tbsp rice wine vinegar

- Soak one rice paper sheet in a large bowl of warm water for about 20 seconds. Gently remove sheet from water. Place sheet on a clean work surface.
- Place 3 shrimps and few chicken strips and boiled rice vermicelli on one side of the rice paper. Place some lettuce, mint, basil, coriander leaves and cucumber on it.
- Shape the filling into a compact log and ensure that you leave about 1 inch of space at the top and at the bottom.
- Fold in ends and roll up firmly to enclose filling. Repeat to make remaining rice paper rolls.

For the dipping sauce

- Mix together sliced chillies and garlic. Add palm sugar and mix until combined. Transfer paste to a small mixing bowl. Add lime juice, fish sauce, vinegar. Whisk together until combined well.

Vegetarian option: Use the same recipe omitting the chicken and prawn. Use soy sauce instead of fish sauce.

Good to know

No fuss dish: No serious cooking involved, barring steaming prawns and chicken. Not a drop of oil. Very nutritious and balanced dish.

Makes 10-12 rolls
Preparation skill level: Easy

SINGAPORE

Eating seems to be the national past-time of Singaporeans. From breakfast till dinner, people seem to be eating all the time. It is said that a Singaporean who moves out of their country, returns back to their homeland because they miss their food the most. From a variety of hawker centres to fine dining, there is never a lack of places to go out and eat in Singapore. It is perhaps the inborn love for food, that eating has become an integral part of every Singaporean's lifestyle. A reflection of Singapore's cultural diversity can be seen in the array of local cuisines on the menu, namely Chinese, Malay, Indian and Noyna (mix of Malay and Chinese) cuisines among others. The national dish is chicken-rice. Other very popular dishes are Singaporean chilli-crab, laksa and otak-otak.

Singapore Chilli Crabs

Stir-fried succulent crabs in a semi-sweet chilli sauce.

2 live mud crabs (Tip: crabs should be used live as crabs start decomposing as soon as they die. The best way to use crab in cooking is to quick freeze the live crab. This makes the crab go to sleep and cleaning and cooking is less gruesome.)

½ cup tomato ketchup

2 tbsp soy sauce

1 tbsp chilli-garlic paste

1 tbsp rice vinegar

1 tbsp sugar

½ cup chicken stock

2 tbsp oil

2 tbsp garlic, minced

1 tbsp ginger, minced

3-4 red chilli, minced (discard seeds to bring down chilli heat)

1 large egg, slightly beaten

2 spring onions, sliced 1 inch long

- Mix tomato ketchup, soy sauce, chilli-garlic paste, vinegar, sugar and chicken stock in a bowl and set aside.
- In a large pan of boiling water, parboil the crab for 3 minutes. Take out of the water and drain. Rinse the crab with cold water and drain.
- Reserve the top shell of the crab for garnish. Remove and discard the gills and the spongy parts under the shell. Twist off the claws and legs; crack them with a cleaver or a mallet. Now, cut the crab into 4 pieces.
- Heat oil in a wok or pan. Add the garlic, ginger, and chilli, and stir-fry for 1 minute.
- Add the crab, and stir-fry an additional 2 minutes. Now add the sauce mix, cook for 5 minutes.
- Stir-in the egg and cook for 1 minute.
- Arrange the crab and top shell on a large platter.
- Pour the sauce all over the crab and garnish with the spring onions.

Good to know

- **Finger-licking:** Eating with finger-tips, rather than the hand, is popular amongst Singaporeans; connoisseurs claim that 'chilli-crabs' had with fingers, make it especially tasty.
- **Chilli-crabs need not be chilli:** Though the name chilli crab implies the dish is hot and spicy, the sugar and tomato paste used, make the dish milder and tastier.

Serves 3-4
Preparation skill level: Moderately easy

Otak-Otak

Fish custard wrapped in banana leaves.

500 gms fish fillet (any white firm-fleshed fish like basa)

10 shallots

2 tbsp garlic, minced

2-4 fresh red chillies (discard seeds to reduce spice factor)

1 stalk shredded lemon grass

1 inch piece galangal

1 inch piece fresh turmeric

2 tbsp shrimp paste, toasted (optional)

Salt to taste

1 tsp palm sugar

2 tbsp oil

1 cup coconut milk

2 eggs

2 tsp rice flour

3 kaffir lime leaves, finely sliced

2-3 banana leaves (cut into 8 x 10 inch rectangles-shaped and soaked in hot water to soften the leaf)

10 betel leaves (daun kaduk), commonly known as paan in India

Serves 6
Preparation skill level: Moderately difficult

- Blend shallots, garlic, red chillies, lemon grass, galangal, turmeric and shrimp paste (if using), salt and palm sugar in a food processor or in a mortar and pestle until fine. Heat oil in a pan and fry the prepared paste till aromatic and oil leaves the sides of the spice mix. Keep aside to cool.

Tip: The above step can be avoided by using 1 tablespoon ready to use red-curry paste.

- Combine ¼ cup coconut milk and eggs. Add the prepared and cooled spice paste and mix well.
- Mix remaining coconut milk with rice flour and finely shredded lime leaves and keep aside.
- Cut out a round circle from the banana leaf. Take a long strip of another banana leaf. Fold along the sides of the outer edge of the cut circle. Secure the ends with tooth-picks. This will form a banana-leaf bowl.

Tip: Banana leaves can be microwaved for 40 seconds to make them pliable.

- Place 2-3 betel leaves at the bottom of the prepared banana leaf bowl. Place a chunk of fish on top of the betel leaves. Pour 2 tablespoons of the chilli paste and egg mixture over the fish. Prepare such banana-leaf bowls and fill in fish and top with custard. Spoon each prepared fish custard with the prepared coconut milk and rice flour mixture.
- In a steamer, steam the fish for 10 minutes over rapidly boiling water.

Vegetarian Option: Use chunks of tofu or paneer (cottage cheese) instead of the fish, and omit eggs.

Ananya's twist:

- The making of the Otak-Otak bowls, involves a cumbersome process. To make things simpler, the fish custard can be prepared in ramekin-moulds or muffin-cups or disposable aluminium foil cups. These small containers are to be lined with strips of cut banana leaves (to bring out the banana leaf flavour) and layered with betel leaves, then recipe follows. This will make the dish from 'difficult' preparation to a relatively easy one.

Singapore Laksa

A coconut milk-based curry soup usually served with noodles, prawns, chicken and bean sprouts. An extremely popular street-food dish.

For the spice paste

2 stalks lemon grass (tender hearts), minced (Tip: discard the woody part of the lemon grass. The soft centre is to be used and is packed with flavours.)

4 red fresh chillies, long and big variety (if unavailable use soaked 4-5 dried red chillies discarding seeds)

2 tsp sliced galangal

1 tbsp grated ginger

1 tsp shrimp paste (omit if you find it strong)

3 shallots, peeled and chopped

3 large cloves garlic

4 tbsp peanut oil (Substitute: If not found, substitute with any odourless oil)

¼ cup fresh coriander leaves, chopped

1 tsp fresh turmeric

1 tsp palm sugar

¼ cup tamarind paste

For the broth

2 tbsp peanut oil

Prepared spice paste

4 cups chicken stock

¼ cup fresh coriander leaves, chopped

¼ cup sweet Thai basil, chopped

¼ cup fish sauce

Remaining ingredients

1 can coconut milk

3 cups cooked vermicelli noodles

1 cup cooked cubed chicken and whole cooked shrimp

For the spice paste

- Combine lemongrass, chillies, galangal, ginger, shrimp paste, shallots, garlic and peanut oil in a blender or a food processor. Blend until well combined. Add coriander, turmeric, sugar and tamarind and process to a smooth paste. (Tip: this spice paste can be prepared and refrigerated for further use.)

For the broth

- Heat oil in a large pan. Add spice paste and stir for a few minutes. Add chicken stock and bring to a boil. Add in coriander, basil and fish sauce and simmer. Stir the coconut milk into the hot broth.
- Place noodles in a large bowl and top with chicken or shrimp and pour broth around noodles.
- You can also top-up with any or all of the following garnishes: bean sprouts, cucumber, Thai basil, carrots, spring onions, coriander, shallots, chilli pepper or chilli sauce. Squeeze a lime over the soup.

Vegetarian Option: Use cubes of tofu instead of shrimps and chicken.

Serves 3-4
Preparation skill level: Moderately easy

HONG KONG

Hong Kong, which literally means 'fragrant harbour', is known for its peculiar marriage of Western and Chinese tastes. This inter-connectivity can be best illustrated with Hong Kong's very own egg-tart – tracing its origin from the western world but significantly different in taste and recipe, adapting to local taste-buds. Hong Kong-style milk-tea is another local favourite, a product of the British colonial rule over Hong Kong. The British practice of afternoon tea, where black tea with milk and sugar is served, became popular in Hong Kong using evaporated milk instead of ordinary milk. Although various cuisines, including Italian, Japanese, French, and American dishes have gained popularity, most locals however, prefer Cantonese-style Chinese food.

Egg Tarts

Wobbly vanilla custard in a buttery pastry tart.

For the pastry

1 cup all-purpose flour
½ cup salted butter
1 tbsp icing sugar
1 egg yolk

For the filling

½ cup fresh milk
¼ tsp vanilla extract
½ cup castor sugar
⅓ cup hot water
2 whole eggs
A pinch of fine salt

Makes 6 egg tarts
Preparation skill level: Difficult

For the pastry

- Cream butter with icing sugar and egg yolk till light and fluffy.
- Add flour and mix well. Press the mixture together and form a dough. Knead well.
- Wrap the dough in a cling wrap and refrigerate for half hour.
- Take out the dough and divide it into 6 equal portions.
- Roll each dough portions into a round disc. Press the disc into individual tart cases.
- Refrigerate the tart cases for 30 minutes.

For the filling

- Mix castor sugar and hot water till sugar dissolves. Let it cool.
- Beat eggs with milk, vanilla essence and salt. Mix in the sugar solution.
- Sieve the mixture and pour into tart shells.
- Bake the tarts in a pre-heated oven at 180°C or 350°F for 25 minutes.
- Usually served piping hot unlike most other tarts.

INDONESIA

Indonesia, the world's largest archipelago, located on an ancient trade route and having rich botanical resources, became the centre of global interest. The cuisine is a reflection of the diverse cultures and traditions. Indonesia's cuisine developed largely as a result of spice-seeking immigrants from all parts of the globe, leaving behind traces of cooking techniques and diverse food cultures. India, China, Middle East, and Europe find influences in its cuisine. *Nasi Goreng, Gado-Gado,* and *Satay* are considered as Indonesian national dishes. Basically there is no one singular Indonesian cuisine. The diversity of regional preparations influenced by the local and foreign culture, is the hallmark of Indonesian cuisine.

Nasi Goreng

Indonesian fried rice with stir-fried vegetables, chicken, fish, prawns and fried egg.

2 cups cooked long-grain white rice (great way to use leftover rice)

½ cup boneless skinless chicken thighs, cut into ½ inch strips

6-8 raw shrimp, peeled and deveined

2 tbsp oil

1 onion, finely chopped

2 teaspoons chopped ginger

1 tbsp dried shrimp paste (optional)

2 tbsp chopped garlic

½ tsp fresh ground black pepper

2 tsp sesame oil

2 tbsp sambal oelek (available in Asian grocery stores. If unavailable use red chilli and garlic paste; but sambal oelek is one of the key ingredient for Indonesian cooking)

1 tbsp oyster sauce

1 tbsp *ketjap manis* (Indonesian sweet soy sauce) (Substitute: Dark soy)

Salt to taste

2 eggs, beaten

3 tbsp chopped spring onions

½ cup chopped coriander leaves, chopped

- Heat oil in a wok. Add the onions, ginger, shrimp paste (if using), garlic and pepper, and stir-fry for 2 minutes. Add chicken and shrimp, sesame oil and stir-fry for a further 2 minutes.
- Add rice and continue to stir-fry for 3 minutes. Mix the sambal oelek, oyster sauce, salt to taste and ketjap manis and stir-fry for 2 minutes.
- Make a fried egg and keep aside.
- Turn onto large serving platter and garnish with the spring onion and fresh coriander leaves and fried egg.

Vegetarian Option: Use shredded veggies like carrots, beans and cabbage instead of chicken and shrimp, and omit eggs.

Tip: *Left-over's paradise:* This is a marvellous way to use up left-over rice. You can mix all kinds of vegetables, noodles and meat available in the refrigerator; toss those up to create this tasty dish.

Serves 3-4
Preparation skill level: Moderate

MALAYSIA

Malaysian cuisine is often known as 'the original fusion food' due to the variety of tastes and gastronomic traditions overlapping one another while maintaining a unique identity. The Chinese influence can be seen from its noodles and the use of soy sauce. Stir-fries and the use of ingredients like ginger, coconut milk and lemongrass are due to the Thai influence. All these and other cuisines, including Indian roti and curry dishes live in delicious harmony in their adopted home. Malacca, the southern Malaysia, is home to delicious Nyonya food which is a fusion of native Malay and Chinese flavours. Penang, on the other hand is famous for its century-old hawker food. *Nasi Lemak* is the country's national dish.

Roti Jala

Lacy pancakes made with coconut milk,
perfect to mop up delicious Malaysian curries.

1 cup all-purpose flour
2½ cups coconut milk
¼ tsp turmeric
1 egg, beaten
¼ tsp salt
2 tbsp oil

Good to know

Handy pancakes: Skilful hands and patience are required to prepare the laced pancakes. When funnels were not available in the olden days to lace the pancakes, banana leaf was used. It used to be quite effective. Some locals can even make it just by using their fingers.

- Sift flour and turmeric into a large bowl. Add egg, coconut milk and salt and mix well to form a smooth batter of pouring consistency (somewhat like a pancake batter), making sure there are no lumps.
- Heat a non-stick pan and brush a little oil. Fill a roti jala cup (a cup with holes to make lace pancakes) (Substitute: If a roti jala cup is not available, a plastic squeeze-bottle with a single nozzle, may be used), until about half full. Move the cup in a circular motion over the pan so that the batter can drizzle out to form a lacy pattern. Cook for 2-3 minutes till set. Slide it to a plate. Repeat until all the batter is used up.
- When cool, roll the crêpe to form a neat tube.
- Served best with a Malaysian curry like a lamb/beef rendang. Well suited for mopping up the curry gravies due to its spongy texture.

Makes 8-10 roti jala
Preparation skill level: Easy

Malaysian Satay (Sate Ayam Saos Kacang)

Chicken Satay - skewered grilled chicken with peanut sauce.

For chicken satay

2 chicken thigh fillets, cut into long strips

1 tsp fennel seeds

1 tsp coriander seeds

2 tsp minced garlic

2 tsp minced ginger

1 handful of mint leaves

1 tbsp minced lemon grass

1 tsp sugar

Salt to taste

1 tbsp soy sauce

2 tsp sesame oil

1 tbsp lemon juice

Oil for grilling

8-10 bamboo skewers soaked in water for 1 hour (Tip: soaking bamboo skewers in water helps to retain heat and does not burn when put under grill)

For peanut sauce

1 cup peanuts

1 tbsp oil

1 onion, chopped

1 tbsp garlic, minced

2 tsp red chilli powder

1 tsp shrimp paste (optional)

2 tbsp fish sauce (optional) (Fish sauce can be quite strong. It contains lot of salt. If omitting fish sauce, add salt to taste.)

¼ cup coconut milk

1 tbsp palm sugar (Substitute: honey or brown sugar)

For the satay

- Thread the chicken into the bamboo skewers.
- Dry roast the fennel and coriander seeds. Blend the roasted seeds along with garlic, ginger, mint leaves, lemon grass, sugar, salt, and soy sauce. Add sesame oil and lemon juice. Marinate the chicken in this prepared mixture for a few hours or overnight. (Good-to-know: marinating overnight helps the spices and flavours to penetrate inside the meat.)
- Brush the bamboo skewered chicken with oil and grill them for 10 minutes or till cooked.

For peanut sauce

- Heat oil. Fry the peanuts and keep aside. Grind coarsely.
- Fry the onion, garlic, chilli, (shrimp paste, fish sauce, if using), coconut milk and sugar. Simmer this mixture for 5 minutes.
- Add the ground peanuts and cook till the sauce thickens.
- Grilled chicken satay can be served with the peanut sauce.

Vegetarian Option: Use paneer or cottage cheese instead of chicken.

Good to know

Satay is such a popular street food, several countries claim satay to be their own creation, and there are several local versions available.

Ananya's twist:

For a delicious alternative, lean beef, shrimp or fish, can be used to make satay.

Serves 4
Preparation skill level: Moderate

BURMA (MYANMAR)

Burmese food embodies a plethora of influences. Burma officially known as Myanmar is a cultural mix, spiced with Indian taste, fused with Chinese ingredients and peppered with Thai influence. Burmese cuisine is an amalgamation of some of the tastiest flavours. Rice and noodles are the foundation of most recipes. Fish or meat are important ingredients along with garlic, lemon grass, ginger, turmeric, coriander, tamarind, chillies, coconut milk, shrimp or fish paste and fish sauce. Myanmar – the fertile stretch of land sharing borders with Thailand, Laos, China, India, and Bangladesh, meets all the criteria for having an amazing mix of different food culture.

Khow Suey

A famous Burmese curry, served with varied accompaniments.

2 cups boneless chicken, cut into bite-sized pieces

2 cups thick coconut milk

Water, as required

2 tbsp gram flour

Oil for frying

½ cup onions, chopped fine

2 tsp ginger, grated

2 tbsp garlic, minced

½ tsp turmeric powder

½ tsp chilli powder

½ tsp cumin powder

1 tsp chilli garlic paste

1 tbsp tamarind paste

2 tsp palm sugar

Salt to taste

Boiled rice noodles to serve with the Khow suey

Accompaniments

Chopped spring onions

Deep-fried sliced onions

Chopped coriander

Chopped green chillies

Fried garlic flakes

Boiled egg, chopped

Uncooked noodles, fried

Peanuts, fried/roasted broken into pieces

Soy sauce

Lime, cut into quarters

- Dry roast gram flour (besan) in a pan and keep aside.
- Heat oil in heavy bottomed pan. Fry the onions till soft. Add ginger, garlic paste. Sauté for 3-4 minutes. Add turmeric, chilli, and cumin powders.
- Add the roasted gram flour, coconut milk and an equal quantity of water, chilli garlic paste, tamarind, sugar and mix well. Add salt to taste.
- Add the chicken cubes to the gravy. Let the chicken simmer till the gravy thickens and chicken cooks (approx 3 minutes).

- To serve, in a bowl first add the boiled noodles, top it generously with the gravy till the noodles are well covered and top with the all the accompanied garnish.

Serves 3-4
Preparation skill level: Easy

Vegetarian Option: Add cubed veggies like zucchini, broccoli, tri-coloured capsicums and tofu to make a vegetable khow suey.

FAR EAST

Simplicity is an adjective you can attribute to Far Eastern cuisine. It is the straight-forwardness that attracts one to this cuisine. As the region is prone to calamities like earth quakes and typhoons, the cuisines have developed using water-based gravy for noodles, soups etc. This cuisine has been influenced by the availability of ingredients and has evolved accordingly. *Kimchi* of Korea, *Sushi* and *Sashimi* of Japan, all symbolises the simplicity that sums up the flavourful yet healthy meals. Characterised by a mixture of meat, vegetables and rice, it serves to be a delight not only for the eyes but also for the soul.

KOREA

It is said that Korean food is all about balance and harmony of mind and soul – mix of sweet and salty, spicy and mild, hot and cold, yin and yang. Although there are similarities in spices and food preparation techniques with Japanese and Chinese food, yet Korean food is quite distinctive. The spicy tang of *kimchi*, the richness of *galbi* (Korean barbecue), and the hearty flavours of *bibimbap* (mixed rice) are very popular.

Kimchi

Pickled cabbage that is extremely pungent. A side dish synonymous with Korean cuisine.

1 medium sized Chinese cabbage
6-8 red chillies, seeded
½ cup malt vinegar
1 tsp minced garlic
¼ cup sugar
Salt to taste
2 tbsp rice wine (optional)
2 tbsp oil
1 tsp red chilli powder

Good to know

Some stories about 'kimchis' are interesting to know –

- It is a very traditional Korean dish, had by the Kings and Queens in the olden days.
- The recipe which was kept a secret amongst the royal gentries got leaked when the princesses sought marriage proposals outside royalty.
- Originally Korean kimchi was made without the use of vinegar but solely by the process of fermentation.

Makes 1 large bowl
Preparation skill level: Easy

- Chop the cabbage into big size chunks and par-boil the same.
- Soak the red chilli in malt vinegar for minimum 30 minutes. Grind the chillies, garlic, sugar, salt and rice wine (if using) to a coarse paste.
- Heat the oil and add to the prepared chilli paste. Add the chilli powder.
- Rub the prepared paste to the cabbage and let it marinate in the paste till overnight.

Tips:

- The dish tastes better, when kept in the refrigerator overnight and consumed the next day, as it absorbs all the various flavours.
- The prepared paste can also be used to marinate chicken or fish or can be used as a hot dipping sauce.

JAPAN

Strange as it may sound – Japanese cuisine uses almost no spices and is characterised by minimalism. A common saying in Japan is – 'the best way to cook, is not to cook'. The emphasis is on purity and clean flavours of the ingredients themselves – fish, seaweed, rice and soybeans. Surrounded by sea, Japan has historically concentrated on making the abundant availability of sea-fish, into a delicacy, if not an art form. Fish is masterfully prepared as *sushi*, and raw-fish is crafted to make *sashimi*. Both have captured the imagination of international foodies – almost any large city around the globe is now serving a healthy and tasty plate of *sushi*, to be dipped into *wasabi* and soy sauce. Japanese food involves the harmony of artistic presentation, together with the unique taste of the food itself. No meal however is complete, without a helping of *sake*, wine made from rice. It is this *Zen*-approach of complete satisfaction to every meal that is so distinctive to its diners, making low-cal and low-fat food, look good.

Chicken Teriyaki

Japanese-style grilled chicken, caramelised to perfection

For the chicken

4-6 chicken thighs with skin on

2 tbsp Japanese soy sauce

2 tbsp dark brown sugar

2 tbsp mirin (Japanese rice wine, similar to sake) (Possible substitute: White wine or white vinegar with 2 tsp sugar)

For the teriyaki sauce

2 tbsp maltose (Possible substitute: Honey, if difficult to obtain)

2 tbsp dark soy sauce

2 tbsp mirin

Good to know

Both mirin and sake are rice wine; while sake is drunk straight; mirin is used mostly for cooking.

For the chicken

- Marinate the chicken thighs in soy sauce, brown sugar and mirin for one hour.

For the teriyaki sauce

- Boil maltose, soy sauce, mirin in a pan until the sauce is glossy and viscous and caramelised.
- Place the chicken thighs, skin side down on a hot grill.
- Grill until brown then flip so the skin side faces up, basting with the prepared teriyaki sauce. Continue basting and grilling till chicken is cooked through and char marks appear in places.

Ananya's twist:

Instead of grilling the chicken, it can be braised in the marinating liquid along with the prepared caramelised honey-soy-mirin sauce. The chicken should be braised till the sauce thickens and coats the chicken in sticky caramel.

Serves 3-4
Preparation skill level: Easy

Tempura

Prawn and vegetables deep-fried in a super light batter.

For the tempura batter

1 cup all-purpose flour

¼ tsp soda bicarbonate

1 cup ice water + as required

1 egg, lightly whisked

For the prawns

6 large prawns, peeled, deveined and tails left intact

Sunflower oil, to deep-fry

Soy sauce, to serve

Wasabi paste, to serve

Vegetarian Option: Use eggplant slices, okra slices, carrots sticks, baby corn etc., and omit egg.

Ananya's twist:

The shells add a super crunchy texture.

Makes 6 prawns
Preparation skill level: Easy

For the tempura batter

- Mix flour and soda bicarbonate and sieve into a bowl. Add one cup ice water, egg and whisk until the mixture is combined (do not over mix).
- Place the bowl over a large bowl filled with ice water. (Tip: place 2-3 cubes of ice in the batter and do not mix. This will enable a super light batter.)

For the prawns

- Heat oil to deep-fry.
- Holding each prawn by its tail, and dip into the batter to evenly coat, shaking off any excess. Deep-fry the prawns for 3-4 minutes or until golden brown. Drain on kitchen paper to get rid of the excess oil. Fry the prawns in small batches.
- Place the prawns on a serving platter and serve immediately with soy sauce and wasabi paste.

Tips: If you do not want the prawn to curl-up during cooking, insert a wooden skewer through the body of a prawn. This will enable to serve the prawns in straightened form rather than the common curled-up structure.

The above is a basic tempura batter recipe. This batter can be used to make vegetable, fish, squid, or chicken tempura.

Maki Sushi

Raw or smoked fish and vegetables rolled in rice and vinegar, covered with seaweed or nori.

5-6 sheets smoked salmon

4 cups prepared sushi rice (recipe below)

4-5 sheets edible seaweed (nori) (available at Asian grocery stores)

2 zucchinis, cut into juliennes

2 carrots, cut into juliennes

1 tbsp marinated or pickled ginger or gari (available at Asian grocery stores)

¼ tsp wasabi, according to taste (extremely pungent horse-radish paste)

4 tbsp Japanese rice vinegar

2 tbsp Japanese soy sauce

1 or 2 sprigs spring onions

2 tbsp roasted sesame seeds

A bamboo mat, to roll the sushi

- Place the bamboo mat on the work surface. Place the seaweed on top on the bamboo mat. Dampen the seaweed with your hand.
- Place a layer of rice on the entire surface of the seaweed leaving out the edges.
- At one end of the sheet place the smoked salmons, zucchini, carrots, marinated ginger and a touch of wasabi.
- Wet the edges with the vinegar again and roll tightly.
- Rest for a while and cut into wedges.
- Arrange on a platter.
- Serve with soy sauce, spring onions and roasted sesame seeds.

Vegetarian option: Sushi can be made vegetarian by omitting the smoked salmon.

Ananya's twist

- Variations in fillings: Try a combination of sliced avocado, omelette strips, deep-fried seaweed, cucumber strips, etc.

For the sushi rice

1⅔ cups sushi rice

1¼ cups water

2 tbsp sugar

½ cup sushi vinegar

- Wash the rice in cold water and drain in a sieve for 60 minutes.
- Add rice to the water and bring it to boil. Lower the heat and cook, covered for 10 minutes. Turn off the heat and let the rice rest for 10-15 minutes.
- Mix sugar, vinegar to rice and mix well to coat each grain well. (Tip: The rice will acquire a sheen when mixed well with the sugar and vinegar.)

Makes 24 cut sushi; each nori can yield 6-8 cut sushi
Preparation skill level: Moderately difficult

TAIWAN

Half a century of colonial rule by Japan and geographical proximity to mainland China, Taiwanese cuisine is a marriage of the two. Emphasis to retain the original flavour of ingredients is the harbinger of Taiwanese cooking style. Light taste and use of fresh ingredients are the main features. Hence, sautéing and stir-frying are widely used techniques, so as to retain the goodness and freshness of the ingredients. Taiwan being an island, seafood is a major focus in Taiwanese dishes. Deliciously cooked prawns or transformed raw fish are Taiwanese delicacies.

Gua Bao Buns

Steamed buns filled with braised pork filling, extremely popular Taiwanese street food.

For the pork belly filling

500 gms pork belly, boneless with skin

2 tbsp peanut or vegetable oil

2 tsp garlic, minced

1 tsp ginger, sliced

2 spring onions, chopped

4 cups chicken stock

2 tbsp soy sauce

2 tbsp Chinese rice wine (Possible substitute: White vinegar)

2 tbsp palm sugar

1 piece cinnamon stick

2 star anise

2 dried red chillies

1 tsp ground Szechuan pepper (Available usually in Asian grocery stores)

2 tbsp hoisin sauce

¼ cup coriander leaves

¼ cup crushed peanuts

For the pork belly filling

- Heat oil in a pan. Sear the pork, first skin side down and then from all sides till lightly browned. Add the garlic, ginger, and spring onions for a few seconds till they become aromatic. Add the chicken stock, soy sauce, rice wine, sugar, cinnamon, star anise, chillies, and Szechuan pepper. Cover and simmer for 45 minutes, until the pork belly is fork tender.
- Cut the pork belly into thin strips and return it to the cooking liquid.

For the steamed buns

- Add sugar and yeast to lukewarm milk and mix.
- Sift salt and flour in a bowl. Make a hole in the centre. Add the milk-yeast mixture and oil and mix to form lumpy dough.
- Place the dough on a floured work surface. Knead well, and cover with a cling wrap for an hour or till the dough becomes double in size.
- Divide the dough into 4 equal balls. Roll each ball into oval shaped flat discs. Grease the oval discs and fold into half.
- Steam for 5-6 minutes till puffed up.

For assembling

- Take each steamed bun. Open up from the fold. Place few slices of pork belly on the bottom half of the bun, and then

For the steamed buns

1 cup flour

2 tsp sugar

1 tbsp yeast

½ cup lukewarm milk

1 tsp salt

2 tbsp oil

top it off with a small spoonful of hoisin sauce, chopped coriander leaves, dusting of crushed peanuts.

- You can also serve individual components like fried onions, beans sprouts, peanuts, hoisin sauce can be placed separately, so that all guests can assemble their own buns.

Vegetarian option: Strips of firm tofu can be used instead of the meat.

Makes 6-8
Preparation skill level: Difficult

PHILIPPINES

Do not be surprised to learn that lizards, snakes, crickets and locusts are consumed in some parts of the world; Philippines for instance. Nothing gets wasted here – an appetiser of crunchy-chewy pig's head and ears (*Sisig*), grilled chicken's heart (*Corazon*), oxtail stew (*Kare-kare*), and there are many others. However, Filipino food would be incomplete without *Adobo* – a cooking style in which meat is cooked in vinegar and other spices. The Filipinos learnt to preserve meat without refrigeration from the Spanish. Latin American and Spanish influences are profoundly present in Filipino cuisine, without being outdone by its Chinese and other Asian neighbours' sway. Due to its various influences, Filipino cuisine is ever evolving and ever changing.

Adobo

Chicken cooked in soy sauce and vinegar. Spanish influenced dish, synonymous with Filipino cuisine.

8 pieces skin-on chicken thighs

¼ cup soy sauce

1¼ cups Filipino palm vinegar (if unavailable use cider or malt vinegar)

3 tbsp garlic, chopped

1 tbsp fresh ground black pepper

1 cup whole canned tomatoes with their liquid

2 bay leaves

4 tbsp extra-virgin olive oil

2 tsp sugar

2 medium onions, thin sliced

2 spring onion, sliced

- Make a coarse mixture of soy sauce, garlic, black pepper, vinegar, tomatoes and bay leaves. Marinate the chicken in this mixture. Cover and refrigerate overnight or longer.
- After marination, cover and cook the chicken for 25 minutes or till done. Remove the chicken from the pan and reduce the cooking liquid till thick. Keep aside.
- Heat the olive oil. Sprinkle the chicken with sugar on the skin. Arrange the chicken pieces skin down to brown, add onions to the chicken and continue to cook till onions are brown. Pour the thickened pan juices over them and serve. Garnish the adobo with a scattering of thin-sliced spring onions.

Tips: Sprinkling the chicken with sugar turns the chicken skin crisp and golden brown.

Serves 4
Preparation skill level: Easy

CHINA 

Chinese cuisine has truly gone global. Indian-Chinese is completely different from what is available in mainland China, and so is Chinese food available anywhere else in the world. Its great tang, ability to adapt to local tastes and retain the goodness of its ingredients has made this cuisine internationally popular. While Chinese cuisine is an all encompassing term, given the very large geography, there are different varieties of cuisines within the same. For example, the south-eastern region is known for its Cantonese (Guangdong) style food and south-western part serves Szechuan (Chongqing) cuisine. While the world may have taken to Chinese food in a big way, it is unlikely that movie goers the world over will replace popcorn with roasted goose wings.

SZECHUAN
A type of cuisine with bold flavours, originating from south-western China.

Kung Pao Chicken

A spicy Szechuan dish made with diced chicken, cashew nuts and chilli peppers.

2 cups cubed or sliced skinless boneless chicken

1 tsp ground Szechuan pepper
(Possible substitute: Chilli flakes)

1 egg white, whisked

1½ tbsp soy sauce

2 tbsp Chinese rice wine (dry sherry) (optional)

2½ tsp cornflour

1 tbsp Chinese black vinegar
(Possible substitute: Balsamic vinegar)

1 tsp hoisin sauce

1 tsp sesame oil

2 tsp sugar

4 tbsp oil

¼ cup cashew nuts

6-8 dried red chillies

5 spring onions, white and green parts separated and thinly sliced

2 tsp garlic, minced

1 tsp minced ginger

Good to know

Going nuts about cashew nuts:

- Cashew nuts are widely used in Chinese cooking; it provides a rich and sweet flavour.
- Cashews are mostly used in stir-fried vegetables and chicken.
- Unsalted cashew nuts should be used for cooking.

- Marinate the chicken with the whisked egg white, 1 tbsp soy sauce, rice wine, and 1½ teaspoons cornflour for 10 minutes.
- Combine the vinegar, soy sauce, hoisin sauce, sesame oil, sugar, remaining cornflour, and Szechuan pepper and mix well and keep aside.
- Heat oil in a wok. Fry the cashew nuts till golden. Drain and keep aside. Add the chillies to the same oil and stir-fry for few seconds. Add the marinated chicken and stir-fry until about 1 to 2 minutes. Add the spring onion whites, garlic, and ginger, and stir-fry for 30 seconds. Pour in the prepared sauce. Stir in the cashew nuts and mix well.
- Scatter the spring onion greens over the chicken and serve.

Vegetarian Option: Use paneer or cottage cheese instead of chicken, and omit egg white.

Serves 3-4
Preparation skill level: Moderately easy

MANDARIN

Beijing cuisine or the cuisine of the capital is the alternative name for Mandarin type of food, originating from the eastern coastal region.

Crispy Duck with Mandarin Crêpes

Inspired by the *Peking Duck*, a crispy roasted duck with paper thin pancakes served with plum sauce, cucumbers and spring onions. Originated in Beijing, now considered as the national dish of China.

For the duck

2 duck breasts with skin

Salt to taste

1 tbsp five-spice powder

1 tbsp oil

1 tsp shredded ginger

1 tbsp honey

2 tsp soy sauce

3-4 spring onions

For the dipping sauce

½ cup hoisin sauce

½ cup plum sauce

For the Mandarin pancakes

2 cups all-purpose flour

1 tsp salt

3 tbsp sesame oil or peanut oil

1 cup hot water, use as needed

Good to know

- Celebration food: Chinese regard duck as a good omen for marital harmony. Served in celebratory meals.

For the duck

- Clean duck breasts. Apply salt and five-spice powder all over the duck. Add oil, ginger, honey, soy sauce all over the duck.
- Place duck breast side up on a pre-heated oven at 170°C or 325°F and roast for 30 minutes till the skin is crisp. Turn duck and roast 30 minutes more. Turn breast side up again. Carve the meat into thin slices.

For the dipping sauce

- Mix the two sauces together to form the dipping sauce for the duck rolls.

For the Mandarin pancakes

- Sift flour and salt in a bowl. Add 1 tablespoon oil, and gradually add the hot water to the flour and mix well. Knead the dough while warm until smooth. Cover and let it rest for 30 minutes.
- Divide the dough into 10-12 balls. Apply oil on the dough balls and roll out very thin circles about 6 inches in diameter. Cook the pancakes on a heated skillet. Brush ½ teaspoon of sesame oil over the top of the pancakes. Use a damp towel to cover the prepared pancakes and keep them from drying out while making the remainder.
- Served rolled with Peking/crispy duck, spring onion slivers and prepared dipping sauce.

Tips

- Do not throw away duck fat. It can be refrigerated and used whenever required.
- Potatoes roasted with duck-fat gives them a delectable flavour.

Tips

- Mandarin pancakes can be cooked in advance and frozen. While freezing, please take care to separate each pancake with a grease-proof paper in between. To be heated before serving.

Good to know

- Versatile duck: Duck meat is versatile. The Italians braise duck with olive oil, garlic and rosemary. The Chinese use five-spice and soy sauce to cook their duck. The French however uses fruits like mandarin, oranges, figs, to cook duck.

Ananya's twist:

- **Make it crispy:** To make the extra crisp duck filling, heat 2 tablespoons of oil in a pan add 1 tablespoon each of soy sauce, honey, 'char-siu-sauce' (Chinese barbeque sauce mostly used for barbequing pork) and few star anise. Add the shredded duck. Cook till the duck spreads are crispy, caramelised and sticky. Throw in some fine slivers of spring onions. Use this filling to roll the crêpes.
- **Continental flavour:** While this is a Chinese dish, you may give it a Continental twist, by marinating the duck overnight in wine or brandy, then roasting it in the conventional way. Then serve it with oranges, olives, herbs and cherries.

Serves 4-6
Preparation skill level: Difficult

MONGOLIAN

The extreme climatic conditions of the northern region of China has influenced this cuisine, reflecting in the prevalence of meat, with less of vegetables and use of minimal spices.

Mongolian Lamb

Stir fried lamb - crispy on outside and juicy on inside.

500 gms boneless lamb, cut into very thin strips

2 tsp minced garlic

4 tsp sesame oil

2 tbsp soy sauce

4 tsp cornflour

4 tsp water

2 tbsp Chinese rice wine or dry sherry

Salt and freshly ground black pepper to taste

Oil for stir-frying

1 tbsp green chillies, finely chopped (chillies can be de-seeded and chopped to reduce the heat)

2 spring onions, cut into strips

1 tsp sugar

Serves 3-4
Preparation skill level: Moderately easy

- Marinate the lamb for half an hour with 1 teaspoon garlic, 2 teaspoon sesame oil, 1 tablespoon soy sauce, 2 teaspoon cornflour, 1 tablespoon Chinese wine and freshly ground pepper and salt to taste.
- Combine 1 tablespoon soy sauce, 2 tablespoons Chinese wine in a small bowl and keep aside.
- Heat oil in a wok. Add the garlic. Stir-fry for few seconds until aromatic, then immediately add the chillies and the lamb. Stir-fry, until the lamb changes colour (1 to 2 minutes).
- Add the prepared sauce. Bring to a boil. Stir in the spring onions. Season with salt and pepper. Add the sugar and 2 teaspoon cornflour dissolved in 4 teaspoons water. Cook till the sauce thickens. Remove from the heat, stir in the sesame oil, and serve.

Vegetarian Option: Use tofu or paneer in place of lamb.

Tips:

- Slice the lambs thinly for rapid cooking.
- Use a sharp knife to cut across the grain of the lamb.
- The lamb will be easier to cut if placed in a freezer 1 hour before slicing as that will make it firm for easy cutting.

CANTONESE

When the world talks about Chinese food, it is usually referring to Cantonese cuisine, originating from the southern part of China or Guangdong province.

Chicken Dumplings

Steamed dough balls stuffed with chicken filling. A popular comfort food.

For the dough

1 cup all-purpose flour

¼ cup hot water

Salt to taste

½ tbsp oil

For the filling

½ cup minced chicken

½ tsp minced garlic

½ tsp minced ginger

1 egg white

1 tsp cornflour

½ tsp sesame oil

1 tsp sugar

2 tsp soy sauce

1 tsp rice wine (optional)

2 tbsp chopped coriander leaves

Salt and pepper to taste

Lettuce leaves, as required

Makes 6 dumplings
Preparation skill level: Moderately difficult

For the dough

- Mix hot water, into the flour. Add salt and oil. Knead to smooth dough. Cover with a damp cloth and keep aside for half hour.

For the filling

- Mix the chicken mince, garlic, ginger, egg white, cornflour, sesame oil, sugar, soy sauce, rice wine (if using), and coriander leaves. Season with salt and pepper till well combined. This makes the filling for the dumplings.
- Divide the prepared dough into 6 equal portions. Roll each portion into thin circles. Place the prepared mince filling at the centre of the rolled flour circles. Fold into a half-moon pouch. Pinch the edges firmly to ensure that the dumplings are tightly sealed.
- Steam the dumplings in a bamboo steamer, lined with lettuce leaves for 8-10 minutes.
- Serve with a soy/chilli dipping-sauce.

Vegetarian Option: Use finely chopped spring onions and tofu instead of the chicken, and omit egg white.

Tips:

- The dumplings can be shallow-fried instead of steaming, or poached in boiling salted water or stock for 2-3 minutes.

MIDDLE EAST

Middle Eastern cuisine has evolved over thousands of years and is known for its aroma, and for being healthy and wholesome. Due to its geographical spread there is a plethora of different types of food and cooking styles. The region has some very special peculiarities – the first course is often treated as a main meal component. Hence, soups and mezzes (array of small appetisers like *hummus, falafel* and *baba ghanoush*) sometimes take precedence; and the magic carpet of culinary delights is just unending.

TURKEY

Perhaps the only country in the world that straddles two continents – Asia and Europe. A mix of Oriental and Byzantine influence, with a touch of Western cuisine, Turkish cuisine has been shaped by history as most other cuisines have been. Coffee is an example of this mix. Introduced to Turkey by the Arabs, the Turkish in turn introduced it in Europe – coffee-drinking, an extremely popular past-time especially among the male folks. There are instances galore of an Arab and European mix in Turkish culinary habits. Charcoal fire is a very popular method of cooking, with Western barbeques acting as an easy answer. *Doner Kebab* (meat cooked on a vertical rotisserie), a Turkish speciality, is a classic example of this east-west influence in the cooking method.

Lentil Soup

A hearty Turkish lentil soup made with red lentils and other ingredients.

1 cup split red lentils
1 large knob of butter
1 large chopped onion
1 large carrot, finely chopped
6 cups chicken stock/vegetable stock
Salt, pepper and cumin to taste

Serves 3-4
Preparation skill level: Easy

- Heat butter in a pan. Fry onions and carrots till soft. Add the lentils and stock, season with salt and pepper.
- Simmer over a gentle heat until the lentils are soft.
- Blend in a food processor till smooth.
- Season with salt, pepper and cumin to taste.
- Serve steaming hot with a lemon wedge, accompanied with crusty bread. This soup keeps well in the fridge for several days.

Imam Bayildi

Eggplants stuffed with mince. The name literally meaning 'Imam fainted', owing to its brilliant taste.

4 medium sized eggplants

250 gms beef mince
(Substitute: Chicken or lamb mince)

Salt and pepper to taste

½ cup olive oil

4 cloves garlic, chopped

2 onions

2 medium tomatoes, chopped

2 tbsp chopped parsley

½ cup tomato purée

1 tsp sugar

½ cup water

Vegetarian Option: Use soya granules instead of the meat mince.

Makes 4 stuffed eggplants
Preparation skill level: Moderate

- Cut the eggplants into half, lengthwise, keeping the stems intact.
- Scoop out (with the help of a spoon) the flesh of the eggplants to create a hollow space. Sprinkle salt and let the juices drain from the eggplants. Set aside scooped eggplant.
- Heat oil in a pan. Add garlic, onion, tomatoes, parsley and minced meat and the scooped eggplant flesh. Cook over high heat for 4-5 minutes.
- Add tomato purée, salt, pepper, sugar and water. Let it cook till the mixture is thick and semi-dry.
- Brush the eggplants well with oil.
- Stuff the minced meat filling onto the hollow of the eggplants, and bake it in a pre-heated oven for about 20-25 minutes.
- Garnish with chopped parsley.

Tip: This process of sprinkling salt enables the eggplants to absorb less oil while cooking and drains out the bitter juices if any, from the eggplant.

Spinach and Feta Gozleme

Turkish flatbread filled with spinach and feta – very popular street food.

1 cup blanched and chopped spinach

½ cup feta cheese, crumbled

- Stir yeast and sugar in some lukewarm water. Let it stand in a warm place or until bubbles form on the surface of the yeast water.

2 cups all-purpose flour

1 tsp instant dried yeast

1 tsp castor sugar

⅓ cup olive oil

Salt and pepper to taste

Lemon wedges, to serve

Makes 4 gozleme
Preparation skill level: Moderately easy

- Place flour in a bowl. Add the yeast mixture, salt and 2 tablespoons olive oil. Knead well for 5-7 minutes to form a soft and elastic dough.
- Divide the dough into 4 parts. Place the dough on a greased tray and cover with a damp towel for 30 minutes or until the dough doubles in size.
- Roll each dough ball into a big rectangle. Place spinach over leaving a margin of 3 inches on all sides. Top with feta and season with salt and pepper.
- Fold dough over to enclose filling and making the shape of an envelope. Press edges together to seal. Repeat making gozleme the same way.
- Heat a griddle pan. Roast the gozleme on both sides with drizzling of oil till golden and crisp.
- Cut gozleme into quarters. Serve with lemon wedges.

Ananya's Twist:

- Spice factor: Add few chopped green chillies along with the spinach feta mix to add that extra kick.
- Flavoured feta and oil: Feta cheese cubes can be stored in an olive oil jar with herb sprigs or garlic cloves which are added for flavour. Feta will acquire the herb or garlic flavour, and will get enhanced shelf life. The aromatic oil can be used for various salad dressings.

LEBANON | IRAN | EGYPT | SAUDI ARABIA | UAE

This vast area, geographically in the middle of world, known generically as the Middle East has similarities in its cuisine and food habits. However every region could have different recipes due to their own particular flavour and style. Middle Eastern cuisines have been influenced by Mediterranean, Arab and Persian regions. Olives and chickpeas are commonly used, and the world's oldest bread, *pita* is extremely popular. Lebanese food has a Mediterranean influence (use of olive oil, nuts, and cinnamon), while Iranian food has a strong Persian influence (lamb gets prominence). The nomadic lifestyle of the Bedouins has touched a few of the cuisines through the presence of dates, almonds and yoghurt.

Chelo Kebab

Flavoured, skewered and grilled meat, served over a bed of rice.
It is the national dish of Iran.

150 gms beef or lamb mince

1 egg, beaten

½ cup onion, finely minced

2 green chillies, chopped

2 tsp garlic paste

1 tbsp Sumac powder ('Sumac' is a berry; used as a souring agent in middle eastern cooking)

½ tsp turmeric powder

½ tsp red chilli powder

½ tsp salt

1 tsp black pepper powder

1 cup coriander leaves, finely chopped

½ cup mint leaves, finely chopped

2 tbsp ghee

Butter or ghee to baste (a cooking technique to add moisture or fat to meat, while grilling or roasting) the kebabs

- Blend the meat mince, egg, onion, green chillies, garlic paste, sumac, turmeric, red chilli, salt, pepper, coriander and mint leaves in a food processor. Place the processed mixture into a mixing bowl. Combine the mixture well with 2 tablespoons ghee.
- Take a lime-sized portion from the meat mixture and make into a ball. Place ball through flat skewers, and shape into square cigar-like shapes. Repeat with remaining meat.
- Place on grill and cook about 4-6 minutes on each side, basting with ghee or butter until meat is no longer pink and is done.
- Serve over a bed of white rice or pita bread; accompanied by middle eastern salads like fattoush (pita-bread salad) or tabbouleh (broken-wheat salad).

Vegetarian Option: Use soaked and boiled kidney beans (rajma) instead of the meat and omit egg.

Makes 6 kebabs
Preparation skill level: Moderately easy

Tips:

- For making kebabs, a mince which has 80% meat and 20% fat, works the best. This keeps the kebabs moist and juicy as opposed to using very lean meat that ends up turning out too dry or hard after grilling.
- The kebab mince should not be washed after mincing and washed prior. Any extra moisture or water will result in the kebabs falling off the skewer during grilling.

Hummus

A dip made with boiled mashed chickpeas, tahini, garlic and olive oil.

1 cup chickpeas, soaked in water overnight and boiled

2 garlic cloves, minced

2 tbsp tahini (sesame seed paste used in middle eastern cuisine)

½ cup water

3 tbsp olive oil

Salt to taste

2 tbsp fresh lemon juice

Paprika powder, as required

Makes 1 large bowl
Preparation skill level: Easy

- Blend the chickpeas, garlic, tahini, ½ cup water, and 2 tablespoons olive oil in a food processor till smooth. Add salt to taste and lemon juice.
- Spoon into serving dish and sprinkle with 1 tablespoon olive oil and paprika powder.
- Best served with crackers, or vegetables such as carrots or celery, or with pita bread.
- Pita bread can be cut into thin triangles, brushed with olive oil and toasted for 10 minutes in a 200°C or 400°F oven to make pita chips, which can be served with hummus.

Ananya's twist:

Add sun-dried tomatoes or roast pumkin purée for variation in flavour.

Falafel

Deep-fried patty made out of ground chickpeas or fava beans.
Extremely popular throughout the Middle East and across the globe.

1 cup dried chickpeas, soaked in water overnight
2 tsp garlic, minced
1 cup onion, chopped
1 tsp coriander
3 tbsp fresh parsley, chopped
1 tsp cumin
Salt and pepper to taste
2 tbsp flour
Oil for deep-frying

- Microwave the soaked chickpeas for 4 minutes. Blend the boiled and drained chickpeas, garlic, onion, coriander, parsley, cumin, salt and pepper in a food processor to a coarse paste. (Tip: Do not process this to a fine paste or the texture of the falafel will change.) Add flour to the mixture.
- Form the mixture into lime-sized balls. Slightly flatten and deep-fry until golden brown (5-7 minutes).
- Falafel can be served as an appetiser with hummus and tahini, or as a main course.
- To make a falafel sandwich, stuff pita bread with falafel, lettuce, tomatoes, tahini, salt and pepper. As an alternative, falafel can be shaped into patties and served like a burger.

Makes 10-12 falafel
Preparation skill level: Moderately easy

Kibbeh

Beef and bulgur-wheat meatballs – very popular street food dish.

300 gms minced beef or lamb or chicken

¼ cup bulgur (broken) wheat (lapsi), soaked in water for half hour

½ cup onions, chopped

Salt and pepper to taste

1 tbsp olive oil

1 tbsp toasted pine nuts (optional)

½ tsp allspice (middle eastern spice mix)

½ tsp cumin

Vegetable oil for frying

- Drain the bulgur wheat dry. Combine it with 1 cup meat, half the quantity chopped onion, salt and pepper and blend in a food processor till a smooth consistency.
- This mixture will form the outer shell. Keep aside.
- For the kibbeh stuffing, sauté the remaining onion in oil. Add pine nuts; add the remaining ½ cup meat. Add allspice, salt, pepper, and cumin till light brown. Allow to cool for 10 minutes.
- Portion out an egg sized amount from the prepared outer shell mixture and form into a ball. Add the prepared filling and seal the edges. Usually kibbeh are oval shaped with two pointed edges. Repeat with the remaining mixture and filling.
- Deep-fry the prepared kibbeh till golden brown.

Vegetarian Option: Use soya granules instead of the meat mince.

Makes 6-8 kibbeh
Preparation skill level: Easy

Baba Ghanoush

A smoky eggplant dip originating in Lebanon and eaten throughout the Middle East.

1 large eggplant
2 tsp olive oil
2 tbsp tahini paste
2 tsp garlic, minced
1 tbsp white vinegar
Salt and pepper to taste
2 tbsp fresh lemon juice

Ananya's twist:

Add yoghurt, chopped onions and pine nuts to the mix to make another popular dip call Mutabbal.

- Smear olive oil on the outer body of the eggplant. Roast the eggplants in an oven or on a BBQ grill for about 30 minutes.
- Peel the skin off and discard seeds. Drain the water from the eggplants by placing them on a colander (a bowl-shaped utensil with holes) or a sieve, for about 10 minutes.
- Blend the eggplants, tahini paste, garlic, vinegar, salt and pepper to taste, in a food processor, till it forms a paste. Add lemon juice and mix and serve.
- Garnish with any/all of the following: olive oil, chopped parsley, sumac spice or chilli powder. Serve cold as an appetiser, with pita bread.

Makes 1 large dip bowl
Preparation skill level: Easy

Baklava

Sweet delicacy made with phyllo pastry, with various nutty fillings inside.
Very popular in Greece and Turkey.

8 sheets ready phyllo pastry (a dough of paper thin sheets; commonly used in the middle eastern cuisine)

1 cup chopped nuts (almonds/ pistachio/walnut)

½ tsp ground cinnamon

½ cup butter, melted

½ cup water

2 tsp rose water

2 tbsp honey

Makes 16-18 pieces
Preparation skill level: Moderately difficult

- Prepare nut mixture by chopping all nuts finely. Add cinnamon powder and mix well. Keep aside.
- Cover phyllo sheets with a damp cloth to keep them from drying out. Butter each sheet thoroughly.
- Place 4 sheets of buttered phyllo at the base of a baking tray. Make a thick layer with the prepared nut mixture on the buttered phylo. Spread evenly. Top the nut mixture with 4 sheets of buttered phyllo.
- Cut the baklava into diamond shape.
- Bake in a pre-heated oven at 170°C or 325°F for 20-25 minutes.
- Prepare syrup by boiling sugar and water for 5-8 minutes. Add rose water and honey. Keep aside.
- Pour the syrup on the baked hot baklava.

Tip:

Baklava should always be cut before baking. Once baked, it becomes very crisp and impossible to cut.

INDIAN SUBCONTINENT

This is a vast region consisting of India, Pakistan, Bangladesh, Sri Lanka, and Nepal. The variety of food in this region is so immense that it is impossible to consider any one particular style of cuisine as typical of the Indian subcontinent. In spite of its large variety, it would be fair to say that this region's food is generally laced with spices and aroma, both vegetarian and non-vegetarian.

INDIA

The variedness of Indian gastronomy cannot be explained in brief. But the aroma of a heady mix of enchanting spices, the addition of chillies to make food spicy-hot, the presence of yoghurt in most recipes and the addition of bright colours set apart this cuisine from the rest. While many follow vegetarianism (no meat and fish) mostly in Western and Southern India, non-vegetarian food is the delight of Northern and Eastern India. The diversity of the regional dishes is so immense that *biryani*, an immensely popular delicacy differs vastly between that of Hyderabad, Lucknow and Kolkata. The fiery *Chettinad chicken* from Tamil Nadu, juxtaposes the heavily spiced and Mughal flavoured *Tandoori* chicken of Punjab. The influence of the Portuguese on Goan food, and the British influences on food habits in Bengal are just some examples of the diversity of Indian cuisine.

Tandoori Chicken

Chicken marinated with yoghurt and spices.
The name comes from the clay oven called 'tandoor' where it is traditionally prepared.

1 whole chicken cut into 4 parts
1 tsp red chilli powder
Salt to taste
1 tbsp lemon juice
2 tbsp mustard oil
1 tsp ginger paste
2 tsp garlic paste
1 tsp green chilli paste
1 tsp garam masala
Red food colouring (optional)
½ cup thick yoghurt
Ghee for basting

Good to know

Traditionally this dish is made in a tandoor or clay oven with charcoal flavour. The taste will surely vary if done in an electric oven.

Serves 2-3
Preparation skill level: Moderately difficult

- Clean and dry the chicken. Make diagonal gashes all over the chicken. Marinate chicken with chilli powder, salt, lemon juice and mustard oil for half an hour.
- Whisk yoghurt with ginger, garlic, green chilli paste and garam masala and red food colouring, and mix well.
- Apply this prepared mixture to the chicken, forcing some mixture into the gashes so that it gets well coated. This time marinate for 6-7 hours. or preferably overnight
- Brush the chicken with some ghee and cook it under a grill for 20 minutes. baste with some more ghee until fully cooked.

Samosa

Fried pastry stuffed with a savoury and spicy filling of potatoes and peas - a popular snack.

For the pastry

2 cups all-purpose flour

½ cup ghee or oil

Water, for kneading

Salt to taste

½ tsp carom seeds (commonly known as ajwain)

For the filling

1 cup boiled, peeled and chopped potato

⅓ cup green peas

½ cup ghee

1 tsp cumin seeds

1 tsp fennel seeds

2 tbsp chopped cashew nuts

2 tsp ginger, minced

2-3 green chillies

1/4 tsp red chilli powder

½ tsp turmeric powder

½ tsp garam masala

2 tsp chaat masala powder

Salt to taste

1 tbsp chopped coriander leaves

2 tsp lime juice

Oil for deep-frying

Ananya's twist:

Instead of potatoes, fillings can be made with crushed peas, cauliflower, paneer and capsicum, spinach, cheese and corn, and lamb or chicken mince.

For the pastry

- Form a pliable dough with flour, ghee, water, salt and carom seeds. Set aside for 10 minutes.

For the filling

- Heat the ghee and add cumin and fennel seeds. When they crackle, add chopped cashew nuts, ginger, green chillies, boiled potatoes and peas and sauté. Add red chilli powder, turmeric powder, garam masala, chaat masala powder and salt and sauté for five minutes. Add coriander leaves and lime juice. Mix well. This makes the filling for the samosas. Keep aside to cool.
- Divide the prepared samosa dough into 10 equal circles. Roll each portion of the circle into thin oval shape. Cut each oval into 2 semi-circles.
- Take each semi-circle. Apply water on the straight edge of the semi-circle. Fold the straight edge, bringing together the watered edges, and seal the watered edges into a triangular pocket. Stuff the potato mixture and then seal the upper edges. Repeat with the rest.
- Deep-fry in oil till golden brown and serve.

Makes 12-15 samosas
Preparation skill level: Moderately difficult

Kulfi

Frozen dairy dessert – the ice-cream of the Indian subcontinent.

2 cups milk (use whole milk for the recipe)

1 can or 400 gms sweetened condensed milk

1 tsp cornflour mixed in 2 tbsp milk

1 tbsp skinless pistachios, thinly sliced

1 tbsp almond slivers

½ tsp ground green cardamom seeds

Makes 8-10 kulfis
Preparation skill level: Moderately difficult

- Pour the milk and condensed milk into a heavy pan and bring to boil over high heat, stirring constantly.
- Continue cooking at a low heat, stirring constantly, until thick and reduced. Add the cornflour milk slurry and mix well.
- Add nuts and cardamom powder. Stir well. Keep aside to cool.
- Pour the mixture into kulfi moulds or small pudding moulds. Cover with plastic wrap or aluminium foil. Freeze until set, for about 6 hours.
- Remove the kulfi from the moulds by running a sharp knife around the edges of the kulfi. Slip each kulfi on to a dessert plate, cut into 3-4 slices, and serve.

Ananya's Twist:

Different flavourings such as saffron, fruit purées, nuts can be added to create variations in taste and flavour.

Vegetable Biryani

A popular rice dish, seasoned and flavoured rice with aromatic spices and vegetables.

For the rice

1 cup Basmati rice

2 each of cloves, green cardamoms, cinnamon pieces and bay leaves

1 star anise

4-5 mint leaves

1 tbsp oil

2 tsp salt

1 tsp saffron

½ cup lukewarm milk

For the vegetables

1 cup mixed vegetable, like carrots, beans, peas, potatoes, cauliflower and green capsicum cut into bite-size pieces

2 large onions, finely sliced and deep-fried till golden brown

5 tbsp oil

1 tbsp garlic paste

2-3 green slit green chillies

1 tsp red chilli powder

¼ tsp turmeric powder

2 tsp cumin-coriander powder

Salt to taste

½ cup thick yoghurt

2 tbsp ghee

½ cup chopped coriander leaves

¾ cup mint leaves

Juice of 1 lemon

Serves 4-6

Preparation skill level: Moderately difficult

For the rice

- Soak rice for 10 minutes. Then cook in lots of boiling water along with cloves, cardamom, cinnamon, bay leaves, star anise, mint, oil, and salt till its half cooked. Strain the water and spread the rice on a large wide platter. Allow to cool. Keep aside.
- Mix the saffron in the lukewarm milk. Keep aside.

For the vegetables

- Heat 5 tablespoons oil; add the ginger garlic paste, mixed vegetables, slit green chillies, red chilli, turmeric, and cumin-coriander powder. Cook for 3-4 minutes. Add salt to taste. Beat the yoghurt well and add to the vegetables. Cover and cook till the vegetables are tender and the gravy is semi-dry. Add prepared *biriyani masala*. Keep aside.
- Spread half of the prepared gravy mix at the base of a baking dish. Spread half of the rice over the gravy mix. Pour 2 tablespoons of melted ghee all over the rice, add half of the caramelised onions and spread over the rice. Next sprinkle a tablespoon of coriander leaves and mint leaves, finally pour about one fourth cup of saffron milk over the rice. Over this layer, spread the remaining gravy followed by the rice. Repeat again with ghee followed by remaining caramelised onions, sprinkle of coriander leaves, and mint leaves and remaining saffron milk over the rice.
- Cover with an aluminium foil and cook in a pre-heated oven at 170˚C or 325˚F for 20-25 minutes.
- Serve hot with raita and papadams.

To make biryani masala

4 cloves

1 inch cinnamon stick

2 cardamoms

¾ tsp shah-jeera (black cumin)

12 peppercorns

Dry-roast, ground and powder the above ingredients.

Kashmiri Rogan Josh

An aromatic lamb curry from Kashmir.

1 kg lamb or mutton, cut into medium pieces
1½ cups mustard oil
1 cup yoghurt
¼ tsp asafoetida
1 tsp dried ginger powder
Salt and sugar to taste
½ tsp cumin
6-8 crushed cloves
2 tbsp Kashmiri chilli powder (Kashmiri chillies render a beautiful red colour without the intense heat)
2 cups water
2 bay leaves
2 tbsp fennel powder
2 inches cinnamon
3 black cardamoms, crushed
1 tsp garam masala
4 green cardamom, crushed
1 tbsp ghee

- Wash the meat and mix with yoghurt and set aside. Heat mustard oil in a big, deep pan. Remove from the flame for 2-3 minutes. Add the meat to the oil and fry.
- Keep stirring the meat till the liquid produced by the yoghurt dries up. Add asafoetida, dried ginger, salt and sugar, cumin and cloves. Continue frying on low flame till it turns brown.
- Add Kashmiri chilli powder and stir till the oil separates from the spices.
- Add water, bay leaves, fennel powder, and cinnamon pieces, crushed black cardamoms and mix well. Cover it with a lid and allow it to cook till tender, on low flame. Add garam masala, crushed green cardamom and ghee and boil it for two minutes. Garnish it with coriander leaves.
- Best served piping hot with basmati rice.

Good to know

Mustard oil has a strong and pungent flavour. Heating the oil at smoking temperature makes it ready to use.

Serves 2-3
Preparation skill level: Moderately difficult

Goan Fish Curry

A tangy and spicy fish curry from Goa.

500 gms fish, cleaned and cut into pieces (use any firm fleshed fish like snapper or surmai or you can use cleaned deveined prawns instead)

1 lime-sized ball of tamarind soaked in hot water

½ cup onion, sliced

½ cup tomato, sliced

1 cup grated fresh coconut

½ tbsp ginger paste

½ tbsp garlic paste

3-4 dried red chillies

½ tsp chilli powder

½ tsp turmeric powder

1 tbsp cumin powder

1 tbsp coriander powder

2 tbsp oil

2 green chillies, slit

2 cups hot water

Salt to taste

- Mash the soaked tamarind well in the water. Strain to extract the pulp. Keep aside.
- Blend the onion, tomato, coconut, ginger, garlic, dried red chillies, turmeric, cumin, coriander and the tamarind pulp in a food processor to make a smooth paste.
- Heat oil in a pan. Add the green chillies, prepared spice paste and fry for 5 minutes. Add 2 cups of water and bring the gravy to a boil. Simmer and cook for 10 minutes. Add salt to taste.
- Gently add the pieces of fish to the gravy and cook for 5-6 minutes till the fish is tender.
- Served best with Goan red rice.

Serves 4
Preparation skill level: Moderately easy

SRI LANKA

Sri Lankan cuisine can be distinguished from a distance. The wafting spice-laden aromas will differentiate a Sri Lankan kitchen from any other. The cuisine has developed over centuries by traders lured by the presence of spices on this beautiful Indian Ocean island. Its closest neighbour, Southern India, especially Kerala, has had some influence over the cuisine. The Dutch and the Portuguese, its early colonisers have also left their legacy on certain dishes, but the British sway is not profound, except in making the country a home for tea-plantations and addicting Sri Lankans to tea-drinking. Bright flavours and overall lightness are hallmarks of Sri Lankan cookery. Use of fresh coconut is fairly common. *Hoppers* (not the insects), which are a kind of crisp flour pancakes (coconut milk is used in its batter), are something Sri Lankans dote on. When eaten with hot coconut fish curries, it leaves a wild and rustic experience of great satisfaction.

String Hoppers or Appa

Lacy pancakes made from rice flour, coconut milk and yeast - a breakfast staple in Sri Lanka.

2 cups rice flour
2 tsp sugar
1 tsp yeast
¾ cup lukewarm water, as required
2 cups thick coconut milk
Salt or as per taste

Tip: To make Seeni Sambol: Deep-fry 2 cups sliced onions till golden and keep aside. Grind the following to a paste: ¼ cup Maldives fish (optional), 1 tbsp ginger root, crushed, 8 cloves garlic, crushed, 3 tbsp crushed red chillies, 5-6 cardamoms, 3-4 cloves, 1 small sprig curry leaves, 1 stick lemon grass, 1 piece cinnamon, salt to taste, 2 tbsp sugar. Fry the prepared paste in oil till the oil separates. Add the fried onions, mix well.

- Add sugar and yeast to the flour. Gradually add ¾ cup lukewarm water, mix well to form a paste. Keep covered and leave it for about 5-6 hours.
- Add coconut milk and salt to the fermented paste, mixing well to form a smooth batter. Keep aside for another 15-20 minutes.
- Heat and grease the appa or hoppers pan. Pour 3 tablespoons of batter in the centre, then tilt and turn the pan in a circulatory way to make the batter form into a circular appa on the pan. Cover and cook for about 3-4 minutes or until it is done. Served best with Seeni Sambol (sweet fried onion relishes) (recipe follows).

Special Utensil:

Special appa pan or a kadai is required. Advisable to get the non-stick variety or else the hoppers may not slide-out easily.

Serves 4-6
Preparation skill level: Moderately difficult

BANGLADESH

Maach (fish) and *Bhaath* (rice) is Bangladesh's staple diet. Bangladeshi cuisine is rich in taste, mostly fried to enhance the tangy flavour of the spices and chillies. However, with the presence of numerous ponds and rivers, fresh-water fish has become its speciality. Hilsa (*ilish*) fish is an icon, found in its most famous river – the Padma. Mustard oil is the main cooking medium. Desserts in Bangladeshi cuisine are based less on milk and dairy (due to inherent shortage of dairy animals), but more on jaggery and rice paste – the delicious *payesh, pithe* and *puli*.

Sorshe Ilish

Ilish (Hilsa fish) cooked in sorshey (mustard) gravy.
The national fish of Bangladesh, with over 100 recipes to prepare this fish alone.

8 medium slices of hilsa fish (ilish)
Salt to taste
1 tsp turmeric powder
1 tbsp black mustard seeds
1 tbsp yellow mustard seeds
4-5 green chillies
4 tbsp mustard oil
2 tsp onion seeds (kalonji or nigella seeds)
2 cups water

Serves 4
Preparation skill level: Moderately easy

- Coat the washed fish with salt and turmeric powder. Keep it aside and let it marinate for 15 minutes.
- Make a smooth paste with black and yellow mustard seeds, salt and 2 green chillies. Add a little water if required. Traditionally it is made in a flat stone mortar and ground with a cylindrical pestle.
- Heat a pan with 2 tablespoons of mustard oil. Add the onion seeds and 2 slit green chillies.
- Add the paste and stir for 3-4 minutes till the paste leaves oil on the side. Next add the fish.
- Pour 2 cups of water. Cover and let it cook for about 4-5 minutes.
- Drizzle 1 tablespoon of mustard oil and 2-3 green chillies.
- Served best with steamed rice.

PAKISTAN

Aroma and flavour are the hallmark of Pakistani cuisine. The classic biryani, made with aromatic Basmati rice, is one of the national dishes of the country. The flavour and aroma of the famous *haleem*, the slow cooked dish of meat and lentils, simply delicious. The Mughals, who ruled the region for centuries, have had the greatest influence on Pakistani cuisine—giving to the world the legendary Mughlai dishes. Perhaps the birthplace of the famed 'tandoor oven', the spiced meat kebabs are absolute delicacies. The famous *Shahi-tukra*, a dessert made from milk, bread and sugar, and flavoured with saffron, provides the lingering tang of satisfaction after a gratifying Pakistani meal.

Haleem

Slow cooked stew of lentils, meat, wheat and barley this is the ultimate comfort food of Pakistan.

500 gms lamb on the bone

¼ cup each split Bengal gram (channa dal), skinless spilt black gram(dhuli urud dal), skinless split green gram(dhuli moong dal) and barley (jau), soaked overnight and drained

½ cup wheat grains, crushed and soaked in water for 1½ hours

5 cups water

1 tbsp garlic paste

1 tbsp ginger paste

2 tbsp ghee

Few strands of saffron dissolved in warm water

1 tsp ground fenugreek

1 tsp turmeric

1 tbsp red chilli powder

1 tbsp coriander powder

1 tbsp cumin powder

1 tbsp chaat masala

Salt to taste

1 cup sliced and fried onions

1 tbsp garam masala

For the seasoning and garnish

Chaat masala

Green chilli, finely chopped

Julienned ginger

Fresh coriander leaves

Sliced lemon

- In a heavy based pan, place the meat in 5 cups of water along with all soaked lentils, barley, wheat, and ginger. Bring to the boil and cook for around 2 hours.
- Remove and discard the bones and continue to cook until meat starts to break down and falls apart (about another hour).
- Add ghee, saffron soaked in water, ground fenugreek, turmeric, chilli, coriander, cumin, chaat masala powder. Add salt to taste. Cook for another hour.
- Add the fried onions leaving 2 tablespoons aside for garnish and garam masala. Cook for a further 15 minutes.
- Garnish with chaat masala, green chilli, ginger, coriander, fried onions and sliced lemon.

Vegetarian Option: Omit the meat and go with the recipe the same way.

Tip:

You can also place the meat along with all the condiments in an oven at 170˚C - 325˚F for 5 hours for the same results. The bones can be discarded before serving.

Serves 4-6
Preparation skill level: Difficult and lengthy

Peshawari Chapli Kebab

The word 'chapli' means flat. A flat meat kebab, traditionally made with beef.

150 gms minced meat (lamb, or beef), made into a paste

1 cup chopped onions

3 green chillies, finely chopped

2 tsp coriander powder

1 tsp red chilli powder

1 tsp black pepper powder

2 tsp garlic, minced

1 tsp pomegranate seeds

1 egg

½ tbsp cornflour

1 cup vanaspati (hydrogenated vegetable fat) (Substitute: Ghee or any refined oil)

1 tsp coriander seeds, crushed (not powdered)

Salt to taste

2 tomatoes, cut into thick roundels

Handful of chopped coriander leaves

Handful of chopped mint leaves

- Mix the following and incorporate into one mass: chopped onions, minced meat, finely chopped green chillies, coriander powder, red chilli powder, black pepper powder, garlic, pomegranate seeds, egg, cornflour and 2 tbsp of ghee or vanaspati. Add the crushed coriander and salt to taste. Refrigerate this mixture for 1 hour.
- Flatten 2 tablespoons of the mixture between your palms to form kebabs.
- Place a tomato slice on top of the formed kebab, pressing it into stick onto kebabs.
- Heat vanaspati or oil in a frying pan. Place the kebabs tomato side down, and fry well.
- Served best with lemon, mint leaves, onion rings and salad.

Vegetarian option: Replace the meat mince with soya granules.

Tip:

Do not use lean meat. Higher fat content in the meat results in softer kebabs.

Makes 10-12 kebabs
Preparation skill level: Moderate

AFGHANISTAN

Difficult living conditions due to mountainous terrain and extreme climatic conditions have influenced Afghan cuisine. Complementing the climatic conditions, Afghan food is not only rich and spicy, but also simple and healthy and usually consists of naan cooked in a tandoor oven, served with meat or vegetables. Afghan food is cooked without exact measurements, and the spices will be adjusted to individual taste. No two Afghans will cook the same dish the same way. Creativity is the hallmark of Afghan cuisine. Food is the centre of Afghan culture – no one comes out of any home hungry.

Afghani Naan

A thin and oval shaped bread, cooked in a tandoor (cylindrical clay or metal oven) – the national bread of Afghanistan.

2 cups flour

½ cup warm water

1 tbsp dry yeast

2 tsp sugar

1 tsp salt

2 tbsp oil

1 tbsp black cumin seeds

Ghee or butter to put on the naan

Good to know

When this dish is prepared at home, it is very difficult to get the traditional tandoor oven taste. But this recipe can just as easily be made in a domestic oven or on a tawa (girdle pan).

Makes 4-6 naans
Preparation skill level: Moderately easy

- Mix ½ cup of lukewarm water, yeast and sugar. Keep aside to 'prove' for 10 minutes till froth appears on the surface. Mix 1 tablespoons flour to the 'proving' mixture and let it rest for 5 minutes. (Good-to-know: 'proving' is a term used in baking where the dry yeast in contact with warm liquid gets activated. This activates yeast and helps the dough to rise).
- Place flour in a bowl, add salt and make a well in the centre. Add oil and yeast mixture. Knead to smooth dough adding small amount of water as required. Cover the dough with a damp towel, and let rise for 1½ hours or till doubled its original size.
- Divide dough into 4 equal parts and roll each one into a ball. Then further roll each ball into an oval shape 6 to 7 inches long and ½ inch thick, sprinkle black cumin and press to stick.
- Apply little water on the naan dough, and place on a pre-heated griddle pan. Roast from both sides. Smear some ghee or butter on top. Alternatively, bake the rolled naans in a pre-heated oven at 200°C or 400°F for 8-10 minutes or until golden brown. Apply ghee or butter on top.

Ananya's Twist:

Add caramelised onion to the dough to make onion naan or stuff with onion, green chilli mixture to make onion kulcha.

NEPAL | BHUTAN | TIBET

The mighty Himalayas, literally meaning the 'abode of snow', and known to be the home of spiritualism by the Hindus and Sikhs, crosses over several countries including Nepal, Bhutan and Tibet. The food habits of this region are typical of high mountainous regions – fewer vegetables and more meat and milk from livestock. Yaks are abundantly found in this region and their very tasty and nutritious milk gets converted into various dairy-based produce including fine cheese and butter. This region has given the world *momos* (steamed dumplings), which are best had with *thukpa* (a soup). If you ever visit the interiors of this region, you would see a common sight of strips of meat hanging outside in the cold for air-drying hence making it bacteria-free. These are then served as crisp and tasty meat chips, eaten raw or cooked. This uniquely different culinary style helps to fuel the sustenance of its people in the extreme climes and geography.

Sel Roti

Nepalese traditional homemade ring-shaped bread made with rice flour – usually prepared during festivals.

1 cup rice flour
1 ripe banana
½ cup powdered sugar
¼ tsp baking powder
Oil for deep-frying

- Mash the banana well. Add sugar, rice flour and baking powder, to make a firm dough. Add a few drops of water if required to make it pliable.
- Divide into 8 equal parts. Take each dough ball and roll into a long cylinder, join two ends to form donut shape.
- Deep-fry the prepared sel roti or donut shaped dough till crispy and golden brown.

Makes 8-10 sel rotis
Preparation skill level: Moderate

Thukpa

A noodle soup which originates in Tibet and is popular throughout the Himalayan region.

1 cup diced chicken thigh fillet

1 cup boiled noodles

1 tbsp oil

5 cups chicken stock

1 tbsp carrots, cut into thin matchsticks

2 tbsp thinly sliced red capsicum

1 tbsp lemon juice

Salt and pepper to taste

Handful of chopped coriander

For the spice paste

½ cup onion, chopped

2 tsp garlic, minced

1 tsp ginger, minced

1 tsp cumin

½ tsp turmeric powder

¼ tsp Szechwan pepper

1 pinch asafoetida powder

1 long green chilli, deseeded, chopped

1 cup tomatoes, chopped

- Blend all the ingredients of the spice paste and process till smooth.
- Heat the oil in pan. Add the prepared spice paste and cook until aromatic (approx. 5 minutes). Pour in the chicken stock and bring it to boil and cook for 10 minutes. Add the diced chicken and simmer gently for 5 minutes, or until cooked.
- Add the carrot and capsicum to the stock and simmer for 2–3 minutes. Add the lemon juice and season to taste.
- Divide the noodles between bowls. Pour in the stock, with chicken and vegetables over the noodles and top with coriander.

Vegetarian option: Use vegetable stock and tofu instead of chicken.

Serves 4

Preparation skill level: Moderately easy

LATIN AMERICA

Latin Americans love their food. Its no wonder that Mexico was recently judged the fattest country in the world. While the food tastes great, it does tend to be rich in carbohydrates. Rice, bread, potatoes and beans are very popular—the Home of Carbs. Mexico, Central and South America form this region, with Mexican food being the rage in many parts of the world, especially in their big brother—USA. An example of rich and tasty food perhaps is best captured by the enticing *empanadas* — stuffed dough, usually deep-fried. The spirit of Latin American life and food is best captured by the term *'joie de vivre'*, joy in everything one does — including the joy of eating.

BRAZIL

Brazil is the land of the *Caipirinha* (the national cocktail drink), *Cacacha* (Brazilian rum), *Copacabana* (housing the famous beaches) and Carnivals. Its cuisines is as famous and tasty. Brazil's gastronomy has been influenced over time by various immigrants like the Spanish and other Europeans. However, the most profound influence on its cuisine is of the Portuguese who colonised Brazil. It is a very large country having differing food habits across the regions, mostly using meat, fish, rice and tropical fruits. Brazil's national dish is *Feijoada* – prepared with pork, and using various parts of its body like the tail, nose and ears. Tourists however do not find the dish very appealing, and hence this national dish remains concentrated within the geographic boundaries of Brazil. Discussion on Brazilian cuisine cannot be complete without mentioning its coffee – the world's largest producer and maker of numerous exotic drinks out of its beans, including adding it to various dishes like *Christmas Turkey*.

Pao de Queijo

Delicious Brazilian cheese bread.

½ cups tapioca flour
⅔ cup grated Parmesan cheese
2 tbsp olive oil or butter
⅓ cup water
⅓ cup milk
1 tsp salt
2 tsp minced garlic
2 eggs, beaten

Makes 6-8
Preparation skill level: Easy

- Mix olive oil or butter, water, milk, and salt into a pan over medium heat till the mixture come to a boil. Remove from heat, and stir in the tapioca flour and garlic. Mix till smooth. Set aside to cool for 10 minutes.
- Add the cheese and beaten eggs into the tapioca mixture and mix well. With help of an ice-cream scooper drop ¼ cup-sized balls of the mixture on a baking tray.
- Bake for 15-20 minutes, in pre-heated oven at 180˚C or 350˚F until the tops are light brown.

Good to know

Tapioca flour has a unique flavour and taste. It can be substituted with buckwheat flour, but the taste will not be the same. Alternatively, as tapioca flour is hard to get, process tapioca pearls (*sabudana*), which are readily available, in a blender or food-processor until finely powdered.

MEXICO

Mexican food is recognised and differentiated by its spicy flavours. Sprinkling of jalapenos on soups, salsas, sauces and even on pizzas – gives the dishes a chilli-kick. Mexicans believe that if anyone wants to know their culture, he must first learn how Mexicans cook. Food is a way of life - it forms one of the most important parts of Mexican culture and conversations. They have contributed several famous dishes to the world. An example is the mouth-watering *enchiladas*, which is *tortilla* (thin flat-bread) rolls filled generally with meat fillings covered with a sauce. The ultimate kick in Mexican fare is a shot of the intoxicating *tequila*. And sometimes the drink may have a worm inside – to provide, perhaps,an additional kick and is said to be an aphrodisiac.

Chicken Enchiladas

Grilled or baked tortillas (thin-flat bread) stuffed with chicken, corn and peas, topped with enchilada sauce and grated cheese.

12 corn tortillas

1 cup chicken mince

2 cups red enchilada sauce (recipe below, can also be obtained in grocery stores)

2-3 tbsp oil

½ cup fresh corn and peas

2 cups mozzarella or Cheddar or Gouda, shredded

Serves 6-8
Preparation skill level: Easy

- Grease each tortilla with oil with a pastry brush. Roast the greased tortilla on a griddle pan.
- Pour ¼ cup enchilada sauce covering the bottom of a 9 inch x 13 inch glass baking dish.
- Prepare the tortilla rolls by spreading 1 tablespoon sauce on the surface of each tortilla. Place chicken mince, corn and peas in the centre along with some cheese and roll up. Repeat with the rest of the tortillas. Arrange them in a line on the prepared baking dish. Sprinkle the leftover sauce and sprinkle cheese on top of enchiladas.
- Place in a pre-heated oven at 200˚C or 400˚F for 15 minutes or until cheese is melted.

To make enchilada sauce

2 cups tomato paste
2 tbsp vegetable oil
2 tbsp flour
2 tbsp chilli powder
½ tsp cumin
½ tsp garlic powder
½ tsp smoked paprika (optional)
2 cups water
Salt to taste

- Heat the oil along with flour and chilli powder. Sauté till the flour is cooked about a minute.
- Add tomato paste, cumin, garlic powder, smoked paprika, water and salt to taste; and cook until sauce is thick and smooth.

Vegetarian option: Soya mince can be soaked in water, drained and used.

Guacamole

An extremely popular avocado dip best enjoyed with nachos.

2 ripe avocados

½ cup red onion, minced

½ tsp garlic, minced

1 tomato, chopped, seeds and pulp removed

2 green chillies, finely chopped

A handful of coriander leaves, finely chopped

1 tbsp lemon juice

Salt to taste

A dash of freshly grated black pepper

Makes 1 big dip bowl
Preparation skill level: Very easy

- Cut the avocados in half. Take the seed out but preserve it. Scoop out the avocado flesh from the peel. Roughly mash the avocado leaving few chunky bits.
- Add the onion, garlic, green chillies, coriander leaves, lemon juice, salt to taste, and pepper, to the avocado-mash.

Tips:

- Leave the seed inside the avocado-mash to retain the lush green colour
- Lime juice is essential in Guacamole. It not only helps avocado from browning, it enhances the flavour of the avocado.
- Seal with a cling wrap to prevent further discolouration by oxidation. Refrigerate till serving.
- Add the chopped tomato to the avocado mix or guacamole.
- Served best with tortilla chips.

Good to know

- Avocado is a fruit, not a vegetable.
- To soften a hard avocado (under-ripe), microwave it for 45 seconds at medium. This will soften it and make it ready to use.

CHILE

Unlike the name of the country, Chilean food is not frequented by chillies, in contrast to Mexican dishes. With its vast coastline, Chile has one of the most fantastic arrays of sea-food. Sea bass is Chile's gift to the world's fish lovers – a fish which absorbs the flavour of any kind of sauce it is cooked in. Chileans are resolute snackers – often spreading arrays of *bocadillos* (little cut sandwiches) to accompany wine and cocktails. *Empanadas* and *humitas*, the lip-smacking snacks, are often had along with a glass of the world famous Chilean wine.

Humitas

Freshly ground corn steamed in corn husks.

2 cups shelled corn (preserve the husks while shelling the corn from the cob)
2 tbsp butter
1 tsp garlic, minced
½ cup spring onions, finely chopped
1 cup shredded queso fresco cheese (Substitute: Blue cheese)
2 eggs
½ cup cornmeal
1 tsp baking powder
10-12 corn husks

- Process the corn in a food processor and drain the excess liquid.
- Heat butter in a pan. Sauté the garlic and spring onions for few seconds and add the butter mixture to the processed corn. Add shredded cheese. Add salt and pepper to taste.
- Add the eggs and mix well. Add the cornmeal to bind the mixture as it soaks up any excess moisture.
- Spoon ¼ cup of the prepared mixture on a corn husk. Fold in the sides and tuck in the edges from all sides to form neat parcels. Use long pieces of the corn husks to tie the humitas or corn parcels.
- Place the humitas in a baking dish covered in an aluminium foil and placed over a basin of hot water in a pre-heated oven at 200°C or 400°F for an hour.

Makes 6-8
Preparation skill level: Moderately difficult

Empanadas

Baked or fried, stuffed pastries with meat and vegetables – a popular Latin American snack.

For the filling

1 cup chicken, diced very finely

½ cup shredded Colby and Monterey Jack cheese (Substitute: Emmental or Cheddar or Gouda cheese)

3 tbsp cream cheese

2 tbsp chopped red capsicum

1 jalapeno, deseeded and chopped

1 tsp cumin powder

Salt and pepper to taste

For the empanada dough

2 cups all-purpose flour

¼ teaspoon salt

¾ cup chilled butter, cut into small cubes

1 egg

3-4 tbsp chilled water

1 egg beaten for egg wash

Vegetarian Option: Use cottage cheese or paneer instead of the chicken, and omit egg.

10-12 empanadas
Preparation skill level: Moderately difficult

For the filling

- Combine the chicken, cheese, capsicums, jalapeno, cumin, salt and pepper and mix well. This makes the filling for the empanadas.

For the empanada dough

- Mix flour and salt in a large bowl. Rub in the chilled cubed butter in the flour and mix with your fingertips so that the mix looks like coarse breadcrumbs. Add egg and drops of chilled water to form a dough. Do not over knead. Refrigerate for half hour.
- Roll out the chilled dough thinly into a large rectangle or square. Cut out rounds, using a 3 inch cookie cutter. Re-roll and repeat procedure with remaining dough making about 8-10 circles. Grease a baking sheet.

For assembling

- Place 1 heaped teaspoon of the chicken mixture in the centre of the round. Fold over the dough, pressing the edges with a fork to seal. Repeat the same procedure with the remaining dough and chicken filling. These forms the empanadas.
- Arrange empanadas on a greased baking sheet. Brush with beaten eggs Bake for 15 -20 minutes in a pre-heated oven at 200°C or 400°F.

Good to know

Brushing with eggs before baking is called egg wash. Egg wash enables the product to obtain a golden brown colour and sheen on the pastry.

PERU

Peru is the potato capital of the world, not only does it produce the largest variety of potatoes but is its ancestral home. Soups and rice are its dietary staples. The vast coast line provides it with one of the widest variety of catch. Over the last five centuries, Peru has absorbed influences from almost every continent and bonded with its native *Incas* – creating perhaps the most original fusion food in the world. *Ceviche*, raw fish marinated over days in citrus juice, which cooks the fish, and served spiced with tomato, onions and pepper, is a famous Peruvian delicacy. Though perhaps least sung about in the world even today, Peru has a remarkable diversity of ingredients; amazing potatoes, wonderful array of fish and a huge repertoire of dishes to satiate the desire of gastronomes.

Ceviche

Citrus-juice cured raw fish salad.
The acid from the lime and lemon 'cooks' the fish without using heat.

2 cups fresh red snapper fillets, cut into ¼ inch pieces (or any other firm fleshed fish like 'barramundi' (bhetki), cod or cat-fish. The fish used needs to be absolutely fresh as it is not cooked in the conventional way. The fresh is cured in citrus juice.)

½ cup lime juice

½ cup red onion, finely sliced

1 cup chopped cherry tomatoes

½ cup cubed capsicum

1 yellow Peruvian chilli, seeded and finely diced (this chilli is a speciality from Peru; Possible substitute: Any fresh red chilli)

Salt and pepper to taste

Few drops of Tabasco

¼ tsp oregano

A small handful of coriander leaves, finely chopped

2 tbsp chopped avocado

- In a bowl, add the fish, onion, tomatoes, capsicum, chilli, salt, Tabasco, and oregano. Cover with the lime juice. Refrigerate for 5-6 hours stirring 2-3 times in between to give it a good mix. This is the method by which the fish is cured or cooked in the acid of the citrus juice). In this marinating process the fish will change its original translucent colour to a white and opaque colour.
- Add chopped coriander leaves and avocado.
- Served best with warm tortillas, or used for making ceviche tacos. Can also be enjoyed with tortilla chips.

Good to know

- **Just have fresh fish:** Classic Peruvian Ceviche does not require any recipe. The only requirement is the freshest of the fresh fish – perhaps just off the boat, lime juice and salt. Spiked with chilli.
- **Modern-day sushi:** Ceviche was introduced by the Japanese immigrants in Peru; no wonder that it is slowly catching up as the sushi of the modern era.

Serves 4
Preparation skill level: Very easy

ARGENTINA

If you want to have the best steaks in the world – Argentina is the place to go to. Argentinean food is rich and usually grilled – a medium used effectively for cooking its ever popular beef. *Ribeye* steaks are an Argentinean speciality, normally marinated with the famous *chimichurri* sauce, which is a mixed herb-paste consisting of parsley, cilantro and oregano. Steaks in Argentina are had in numerous ways and are in fact the national dish. For those with a sweet tooth, *Dulce de Leche*, (literally meaning 'the milk-candy'), is the most common Argentinean dessert preparation. It makes a sweet ending to the otherwise spiced-up steaks.

Dulce de Leche

Milk candy made from slow cooked condensed milk.

1 can sweetened condensed milk

Makes 1 large bowl
Preparation skill level: Very easy

- Place the condensed milk can on a deep baking dish. Pour enough hot water to the dish so that it reaches halfway up the sides of the condensed milk can.
- Bake in a pre-heated slow oven at 130˚C or 250˚F for 2 hours. (A note of caution: The tin might crack or bend due to the heat.)
- Cool the can completely. The condensed milk will be caramelised and the consistency will turn similar to thick peanut butter.
- Dulce de leche is extremely versatile and can be used as toppings for ice-cream, cakes, pastries and donuts.

USA

America, known as 'the melting pot of the world' – is where different cultures and ethnicities, together have produced diverse cuisines. While *Clam chowder* (sea-food soup) from the North-East is famous, Southern cooking is synonymous with barbeques and deep-fried chicken. In the heart of the South, Creole and Cajun cuisine is a superb mix of Spanish and French style cooking flavoured with African and West Indian hot spices and pepper. Move to the South-West and you will find the home of salsas, nachos and tacos. Tex-Mex cuisine originates from this region - Texas and along the Mexican border. Travel west to California, which is the home of experimental cuisine. Given the diversity in this vast country, it is difficult to say, what American food is – but hamburgers, hotdogs and chicken wings will always be known to be America's contribution to the world of fast-foods. Americans love to eat good food – no wonder seven of the world's top fifty restaurants are in USA, only to be matched by Spain.

Cajun Blackened Fish

Marinated and spice rubbed fish, seared on a smoking hot pan for the blackened effect.

6 fillets of any firm fish (for variation you can use chicken breast fillets too)

2 tbsp paprika

2 tbsp lime zest

2 tsp garlic powder

2 tsp black pepper

1 tsp dried basil

1 tsp onion powder

1 tsp thyme

Salt to taste

1 cup unsalted butter, melted

- Heat a cast iron skillet (recommended as the black charred colour will come from cooking food on cast iron) or any heavy skillet over high heat.
- Prepare a spice mix by mixing together paprika, lime zest, garlic powder, pepper, basil, onion powder, thyme, and salt to taste. Dip fish fillets into melted butter and coat both sides of fish with the prepared spice mixture.
- Place the spice rubbed fillets on the hot skillet.
- Baste each fillet with 1 teaspoon melted butter.
- Cook over high heat for about 2 minutes on each side till fish flakes easily and the skin is charred and blackened.

Serves 3
Preparation skill level: Moderately easy

All-American Cheesecake

Most popular American dessert made with soft cream-cheese, on a base crust made with cookies or biscuits. This is an eggless, no-bake cheesecake.

20 Oreo cookies

1½ cups or 250 gms cream cheese (e.g. Kraft's Philadelphia cream cheese)

2-3 tbsp melted butter

1 tbsp gelatine

⅓ cup sugar

⅓ cup fresh thick cream

½ tsp vanilla extract

Serves 4-6
Skill level: easy

- Blend ten Oreo cookies and the melted butter into a coarse powder. Press this mixture firmly into the base of a cheesecake tin. Refrigerate until set.
- Stir the gelatine in water and microwave for 1 minute or cook over a double boiler (i.e. cooking over indirect heat), till well dissolved and forms into a translucent liquid. Keep aside.
- Blend the cream cheese, sugar, fresh cream, and vanilla extract in a blender till well mixed. Add the gelatine mixture and mix. Break 5-6 Oreo cookies each into small bits and combine in the cheese mixture.
- Take the refrigerated set Oreo crumbs, pour the cream cheese mixture over it and refrigerate again for a good 4-5 hours or till set.
- Decorate the top with the remaining cookies.

Good to know

New York style cheesecake: There are many ways of making cheesecakes. One commonly used technique is to 'bake' the cheesecake. The cream cheese is mixed with condensed milk and eggs. This is baked on a base of biscuits or cookie crumbs. The famous New York style cheesecake is a baked cheesecake.

Ananya's Twist:

- You can make different flavoured cheesecake by adding seasonal fruits or fruit purées, like strawberries, mangoes and peaches.
- You can substitute the Oreo cookies by using Digestive-biscuits or Crackers, for a taste variation.

Pecan Pie

A scrumptious pie with a filling of caramelised pecan nuts.

For the pie crust

1 cup flour

2 tbsp castor sugar

½ cup chilled butter, chopped

1 egg, beaten

Extra flour, for rolling the dough

For the filling

2 cups chopped toasted pecans (if unavailable, use walnuts)

5 tbsp butter

1 cup brown sugar

¾ cup corn syrup

1-2 tbsp bourbon (optional)

2 tsp vanilla extract

3 beaten eggs

Serves 4-6
Preparation skill level: Moderately difficult if making the pastry from scratch.

For the pie crust

- Prepare the dough by mixing together the flour and sugar. Mix in the chilled butter using finger tips into the dry ingredients until the mixture resembles coarse breadcrumbs. Add the egg and bring the dough together, sprinkle a few drops of cold water if the mixture looks dry. Wrap the dough in cling wrap and refrigerate for an hour.
- On a floured work top, roll out the dough into a round or rectangle. Transfer the dough to a 12 inch rectangular or 9 inch round pie pan. 'Blind bake' the prepared pie shell. (Blind-baking involves: Put a piece of parchment paper or foil over the pie shell and fill with dried beans or pie weights. Bake till the dough is set, for about 20 minutes. Remove from the oven and lift sides of the parchment paper to remove the beans.) Bake for a further 10 minutes till the pie shell is golden.

For the filling

- Boil the butter, brown sugar and corn syrup stirring constantly. Remove from the heat and add in the nuts, bourbon, and the vanilla. Whisk in beaten eggs to the prepared mixture and pour the filling into the prepared crust.
- Bake in a pre-heated oven at 180°C or 350°F for about 45 minutes till the filling looks set and golden.

Meat Loaf

Mince meat with various condiments, baked in a loaf tin.

2 cups minced beef or lamb (traditionally half beef and half pork is used)

2 tbsp butter

1 onion, chopped

1 tbsp garlic, chopped

1 stick celery, finely chopped

1 cup breadcrumbs

1 cup milk

2 eggs, beaten

2 tbsp chilli sauce

2 tbsp Worcestershire sauce

3 boiled eggs

Salt pepper to taste

6-8 bacon rashers (strips)

Serves 3
Preparation skill level: Moderately easy

- Melt butter in a pan. Add onion, garlic, celery and sauté till onions softens. Keep the mixture aside.
- Soak the breadcrumbs in the milk. (Good-to-know: Addition of soaked breadcrumbs in milk, makes the meat loaf very moist and succulent). Set aside.
- Mix together minced meat, the prepared onion-garlic mixture, beaten eggs, chilli sauce, and Worcestershire sauce, breadcrumbs soaked in milk, salt and pepper. Mix well. Place ½ the mixture in a loaf tin, place 3 boiled eggs in a line over the mince. Cover them completely with the remaining mince to form a neat bread loaf like structure.
- Lay the bacon rashers across the meat loaf tucking in the edges.
- Bake in a pre-heated oven for one hour at 170°C or 325°F, basting occasionally with meat juices and bacon fat droplets that fall in the pan. Let the loaf rest and cool down.
- Cut into slices and serve.

Ananya's Twist:

Mashed potato topped meat loaf: 20 minutes before the meat loaf is done, cover it with a layer of mashed potatoes, with thickness of one inch. Brush the mashed potatoes with olive oil or melted butter, and half cup of grated cheese. Finish it in the oven for 20 minutes. The meat loaf will have a lovely layer of crisped potatoes. It's a variation from the regular meat loaf preparation.

CANADA 

The Canadian national flag is adorned with the maple leaf in its centre. It depicts how important maple is for the Canadians. Nothing compares with the delicious taste of crispy bacons dipped in luscious maple syrup, but there is much more to Canadian cuisine than just maple. Canada, being an immigrant country celebrated for its diversity has developed a cuisine through the inter-mingling of immigrant cooking habits and culture. An example of such a marriage is the popular *Poutine* – regular French fries served with cheese sauce. *Dulce de Leche Sticky Buns*, a mix of South American milk-candy, served on buns, is another example of the fusion-food Canada has to offer.

Poutine

French fries topped with cheese sauce.

3 potatoes cut into French fries and soaked in water

1 cup cream cheese

1 tbsp oil

1 tbsp butter

1 onion, finely chopped

1 tsp garlic, minced

2 tbsp tomato ketchup

1 tbsp vinegar

½ tsp Worcestershire sauce

Vegetable oil for frying

Salt and pepper to taste

Serves 4
Preparation skill level: Moderately easy

- Heat oil and butter in a pan. Sauté the onion and garlic for 2-3 minutes. Add ketchup, vinegar, Worcestershire sauce and simmer on medium heat. Add cream cheese and mix well. Keep aside.
- Drain the cut potatoes and dry them well. Deep-fry until golden. Drain them in a kitchen towel. Add salt and pepper. Pour prepared sauce on top. Best served piping hot.

Good to know

Poutine is both, served in fast-food restaurants as well as fine dining ones. Poutine is even served with the expensive foie-gras.

Tip:

Though a bit of extra work, to make the potatoes extra crisp from outside and gooey soft from inside, fry the potatoes in low temperature oil till it is just done. Drain it and keep it aside. Just before serving, re-fry the potatoes at a high temperature, to make the exterior golden. It will be a delicious version.

Pain Perdu

French toast dusted with confectioners' sugar and fresh berries. 'Pain Perdu' literally means 'lost bread'. It's a good way of using day-old bread that would otherwise be wasted.

4 thick slices of day-old bread
2 eggs
2 tbsp castor or ground sugar
1 cup milk
2 tbsp vanilla extract
2 tbsp butter
Whipped cream, powder sugar, or berries for garnish

- Beat the eggs, sugar and milk very well. Add vanilla extract to the mixture. Soak the slices of bread into the egg mixture, to coat from all the sides. Keep soaked for 10 minutes.
- Melt the butter in a large pan. Cook the soaked bread slices for 3 minutes on each sides, until they are golden brown and crisp at the sides.
- Sprinkle with powdered sugar, whipped cream. Garnish with berries.

Serves 4
Preparation skill level: Moderately easy

CARIBBEAN ISLANDS

From Grenada to St. Vincent, from Trinidad and Tobago to Dominica, this group of small islands is home to one of the most fun-loving people. The West Indies Islands, another name for the Caribbean Islands, has more to offer than just calypso, carnival and cricket. Its cuisine is a cultural patch-work of the various islands gifted with bountiful of natural ingredients. Nature's bounty is unending – home to some of the best cocoa produced in the world, coffee in the mountainous Jamaica, vast sugar-cane fields in Trinidad and Barbados, and sweet pineapples of the Dominican Republic.

JAMAICA

A visit to the islands will be incomplete without sampling the superb Jamaican-style Jerk Chicken spicy and full of flavour – truly reflecting the ethos of the food-loving inhabitants.

Barbecued Jerk Chicken

Chicken barbequed with a jerk spice rub.
Jerk is a blend of herbs and spices, used on meat, before roasting.

2 whole chicken legs (drumsticks and thigh)

2 spring onions, finely chopped

1 tsp minced garlic

1 tbsp lime juice

4 tbsp olive oil

1 tsp thyme

1 tsp allspice powder (Jamaican spice mix)

1 tsp chilli powder

3-4 green chillies (discard the seeds to reduce the chilli heat)

Salt and pepper to taste

¼ tsp nutmeg powder

- Mix together the spring onions, garlic, lime juice, 2 tablespoons olive oil, thyme, allspice powder, chilli powder, nutmeg powder and green chillies. Season with salt and pepper. Combine to form a uniform paste.
- Make gashes or incisions on the chicken legs. Rub-in the mixed paste, making sure the paste gets into all slits and crevices. Cover and refrigerate for 6-8 hours or preferably overnight.
- Place the chicken, under a pre-heated grill for ½ hour or on a barbeque, basting with oil and turning 4-5 times in between.
- Chicken is ready to serve.

Tip:

Charcoal-based flame gives a unique flavour to the dish.

Serves 2
Preparation skill level: Moderately easy

AUSTRALIA AND NEW ZEALAND

The most popular ANZAC (short form for Australia and New Zealand Army Corps) biscuits truly reflects the collaboration between these twin countries lying far-off in the Pacific Ocean. Known for its long shelf life, the biscuits, were made by the A&NZ wives during World War One for their hubbies fighting the battle. The cuisine of this region is a blend of the original Aboriginals and the 18th century European settlers. Bush-tucker is a good example of this. Adapted even in the modern cuisine, it uses crocodile, kangaroo, insects (nutty-tasting grub) and bugs as standard ingredients. To sight some iconic foodstuffs, *macadamia nuts* are a good example of high commercialisation of this national produce. *Vegemite,* the dark-brown local bread spread (looks a lot like UK's Marmite), is a local rage though not liked much by visitors. This region's cuisine is home to the old style of cooking as well as modern day trends – fusion food, at its best.

Macadamia Nut-Crusted Barramundi

Batter-fried barramundi (the most popular fish found in the Australian coastline) with a macadamia-nut (most popular Australian nut) crust.

4 barramundi fillets (Possible substitute: Any firm fleshed fish)

2 cups roasted macadamia nuts (Possible substitute: Almonds)

1 cup fresh breadcrumbs

Salt and pepper to taste

2 eggs, lightly beaten

¼ cup olive oil

lemon wedges

Vegetarian Option:

Use paneer or cottage cheese slices instead of the fish.

- Process the macadamia nuts to coarse crumbs in food processor. Mix with the fresh breadcrumbs and season with salt and pepper.
- Beat the egg well. Dip both sides of fish fillets into egg mixture and further coat with the breadcrumb mixture, Transfer on to a plate. Cover and refrigerate for half hour.
- Heat oil in a non-stick pan. Cook the crumbed fish for 3 to 4 minutes on each side or till golden in colour.
- Served best with lemon wedges, aioli and salad.

Serves 4
Preparation skill level: Moderately easy

Lamingtons

Vanilla sponge cake, cut into cubes, dipped in sweet chocolate frosting with coconut sprinkling around it.

For the sponge

2 cups or 300 gms all-purpose flour

½ cup or 125 gms butter

2 cups or 300 gms castor sugar

4 large eggs

2 tsp pure vanilla extract

2 tsp baking powder

½ cup milk

For the chocolate coconut frosting

⅓ cup cocoa powder

1 cup desiccated coconut

2 cups icing sugar

3 tbsp butter

½ cup milk

Tip:

If you use a store bought sponge, the recipe becomes incredibly easy.

Makes 12-16 lamingtons
Preparation skill level: Moderately difficult

For the sponge

- Cream the butter and sugar well in a food processor until pale and fluffy. Add one egg at a time to the butter/sugar mixture. Beat very well after each addition. Add vanilla extract and mix well.
- Sift flour and baking powder. Fold the flour in to the butter egg mixture. Add milk and combine well. Spread the batter evenly into a greased cake tin.
- Bake in a pre-heated oven at 180˚C or 350˚F for 30 minutes or till a toothpick comes out clean when inserted in the middle of the cake.
- Cool the cake completely. Cut it into squares and refrigerate for at least 2-3 hours.

For the chocolate coconut frosting

- Place the icing sugar, cocoa powder, butter and milk in a double boiler. Stir till the mixture is smooth and thick. Keep aside.
- Coat the prepared sponge cake squares on all sides in the icing mixture and then gently roll the cake in desiccated coconut. Repeat the process for all the cake squares.

Vegetarian Option: Use eggless sponge (stores-bought) and follow the recipe.

Pavlova

A dessert made of meringue filled with whipped cream
and fresh fruit - considered a favourite in Australia and New Zealand.

4 egg whites
A pinch of salt
1 cup castor sugar
1 tsp vinegar
2 tsp cornflour
2 cups whipped cream
Assorted fruit to decorate

Tips:

- A test to see if the meringue is done is to invert the bowl and check that it does not fall off, but yet holds stiff and forms a peak.
- Humidity causes the sugar to absorb moisture to make the meringue soft; adding the cornflour prevents this from happening.

Good to know

Beating the egg whites at a high speed, and then adding one tablespoon of sugar at a time, makes the meringue very glossy and stiff.

- On a greaseproof butter paper, draw a circle of 20 cm diameter. Brush with oil on the surface of the paper and place on an oven tray. Keep aside.
- In a food processor, beat egg whites and salt at a very high speed until it forms a stiff peak. Add sugar, 1 tablespoon at a time, beating really well after each addition. The meringue changes its texture and becomes smooth and glossy, and hold firm peaks.
- Fold in the vinegar and cornflour to the meringue mixture.
- Spoon the mixture onto the prepared greased paper circle and spread evenly on the circle.
- Bake for 1½ hours in a cold oven (not pre-heated) at 130° C or 250°F. After 1½ hours let the pavlova/meringue cool in the oven.
- Cover with whipped cream and decorate with strawberries, sliced kiwi fruit or passion fruit to serve.

Serves 4
Preparation skill level: Moderate

Anzac Biscuits

Special long-lasting biscuits made with oats and brown sugar.

1 cup oats

1 cup brown sugar

1 cup flour

½ cup grated coconut (fresh is preferred but desiccated would also do)

125 gms butter

2 tbsp golden syrup

1 tbsp water

½ tsp soda bicarbonate

- Sift the flour and add sugar, oats and coconut. Combine well. Keep aside.
- Melt the butter in a pan and add golden syrup and water. Stir in the soda bicarbonate into the butter mixture.
- Add the prepared liquid to the prepared flour-oats mixture and mix well.
- Place small lime-sized balls from the mixture on a greased tray and bake in a pre-heated oven at 185°C or 350°F for 15-20 minutes.
- Cool on a wire rack and store in an airtight container.

Makes 8-10
Preparation skill level: Moderately easy

Good to know

Vegetarian Non-Vegetarian

MEAT
(LAMB, BEEF, PORK)

- When buying meat, preferably get meat with the bones, rather than boneless. Meat with bones, retain more flavour.
- If the recipe calls for boneless meat then cut the meat from the bones. The bones can be used to make meat-stock.
- To make meat stock, aromatics like ginger, garlic, carrot, celery, onions can be added with plenty of water. Boil for 2-3 hours. Strain. Use the clear stock for further cooking. This home-made stock will have a fabulous flavour.
- It is always good to sear the meat. Searing involves placing tossing on a very hot pan, so that the outer meat cooks well to retain all the juices inside.
- Marinating meat with acids (like, white wine, vinegar, yoghurt, lime juice) makes the meat tender. Grated papaya is also a great meat tenderiser.

FISH

BUYING TIPS

- While buying fish, ensure that the fish is firm to touch, scales and eyes are bright. Sulking eyes means the fish is stale. The gills to be deep red colour.
- Fish should look shiny and moist, as if it has just come out of water. If the fish has dry hard skin, it means it is stale.
- Fish should smell of the water it has come from. For sea-fish, it should have the smell of the sea. Fishy odour from fish means something fishy.

COOKING TIPS

- Fish or any seafood, should not be over-cooked. Or else it will become tough and rubbery.
- Cook fish up to a point where it can flake by a spoon, easily.
- Do not discard shells of prawns and lobsters. The discarded shells can be sautéed in aromatics (like ginger, garlic, herbs), crushed or puréed, and strained. The resultant stock will help to add superb flavour to soups, stews and other fish preparations.

WINE OR ALCOHOL IN FOOD

- Do not cook anything with a wine or alcohol which you will not drink.
- Any left-over wine should be re-corked, refrigerated and used for cooking or marinating.
- Wine or alcohol should not overpower the essence of the main dish – it should complement it.
- Wine is very good for deglazing pans. After the meat is roasted or food is cooked, the brown residue can be splashed with some wine. Stir. It will loosen the brown parts. A thick and flavourful sauce will form. Pour it over the cooked dish.
- When food is cooked with wine or alcohol for 15-20 minutes, the spirit in the alcohol evaporates. Leaving behind a subtle aroma or flavour.

MEASUREMENTS

QUANTITY	WEIGHT
1 cup flour, cornflour, castor sugar, icing sugar, cocoa powder	150 gms
1 cup grain sugar	220 gms
1 cup lentils	165 gms
1 tbsp flour	10 gms
1 tbsp grain sugar	16 gms

QUANTITY	WEIGHT
1 cup	250 ml
½ cup	125 ml
⅓ cup	70 ml
¼ cup	60 ml

TEMPERATURE CHART

GAS MARK	FAHRENHEIT	CELSIUS	DESCRIPTION
Quarter (1/4)	225	110	Very cool/very slow
Half (1/2)	250	130	-
1	275	140	cool
2	300	150	-
3	325	170	very moderate
4	350	180	moderate
5	375	190	-
6	400	200	moderately hot
7	425	220	hot
8	450	230	-
9	475	240	very hot